TEXAS BIOGRAPHICAL DICTIONARY

LYNDON B. JOHNSON

TEXAS
BIOGRAPHICAL
DICTIONARY

PEOPLE OF ALL TIMES AND ALL PLACES
WHO HAVE BEEN IMPORTANT TO THE HISTORY
AND LIFE OF THE STATE

American Historical Publications, Inc.
725 Market Street
Wilmington, Delaware 19801

ISBN

0-937862-54-1

A

•**ABBOTT, JO (JOSEPH)**, (1840-1908)- U. S. Representative, was born near Decatur, Morgan County, Ala., January 15; attended the public schools; moved with his parents to Freestone County, Texas, in 1853; during the Civil War served in the Confederate Army as first lieutenant in the Twelfth Regiment, Texas Cavalry; studied law; was admitted to the bar in 1866 and commenced practice in Springfield, Limestone County, Texas; subsequently moved to Hillsboro and continued the practice of law; member of the State house of representatives in 1870 and 1871; appointed district judge of the twenty-eighth judicial district by Governor Roberts in February 1879; subsequently elected in November 1880 for a term of four years; elected as a Democrat to the Fiftieth and to the four succeeding Congresses (March 4, 1887-March 3, 1897); was not a candidate for renomination in 1896; resumed the practice of law in Hillsboro, Hill County, Texas and died there February 11.

•**ALGER, BRUCE REYNOLDS**, (1918-)- U. S. Representative, was born in Dallas, June 12; moved to Webster Groves, Mo., with his parents in 1924, and attended the public schools; graduated from Princeton University, Princeton, N. J., in 1940; field representative with RCA Victor Manufacturing Co., 1940 and 1941; enlisted as an aviation cadet in the Army Air Corps in September 1941, served as a B-29 commander in the Pacific Area, and discharged in November 1945; returned to Dallas, Texas, and engaged in the real-estate and construction business; elected as a Republican to the Eighty-fourth and to the four succeeding Congresses (January 3, 1955-January 3, 1965); unsuccessful candidate for reelection in 1964; resumed real estate pursuits; is a resident of Boca Raton, Fla.

6

•ALLRED, JAMES V. (1889-1959), thirty-second governor of Texas (1935-39), was born in Bowie, Texas, the son of *Renne and Mary Hinson Allred*. He attended public school, and received an L.L.B. from Cumberland University in 1921, after a brief term at the Rice Institute. He joined the U.S. Navy during World War I, but returned to his hometown to practice law after the War. He was elected district attorney for his area in 1923, and then returned to a private practice in 1926. Five years later he was elected Attorney General of Texas. When *Governor Ferguson* decided not to run for a third term, Allred was easily nominated and elected to her seat. When he took office in January 1935, the Depression had wrought large changes in the state government. Voters and the legislature continued to approve new programs to help the needy; unemployment insurance, old age assistance, and farm relief, but no new taxes were approved. Twelve new boards and commissions had been created to carry out the relief programs, but no new money was coming in to meet continued payments. When Allred sought reelection in 1936, pensions and taxes were the key issues of the day, and the governor advocated pensions only for elderly persons who really needed it, while asking for few new taxes. He was reelected by a large majority. However, Allred was forced to appeal to the legislature for additional revenue. The lawmakers refused to raise taxes on oil, gas and sulphur, and they repealed a law allowing betting on horseracing, which had been a rich source of revenue since 1933. However, liquor taxes helped the state make its pension obligations, and the federal government provided some assistance. In 1936, Allred presided over the Texas centennial celebrations, which were held at Dallas and various historical places in the state. When Allred left office, he was appointed by *President Roosevelt* to become a federal district judge. He resigned in 1942 when he ran for U.S. Senator, but was unsuccessful. *President Truman* reappointed Allred to his former judgeship in 1949, and he served there until his death. His grave is in Wichita Falls.

•ANDREWS, MICHAEL ALLEN, (1944-)- U. S. Representative, Democrat, of Houston, Texas; was born in Houston, February 7; attended the public schools of Fort Worth, Texas, graduated from

Arlington Heights High School, 1962; B.A., University of Texas, Austin, Texas, 1967; J.D., Southern Methodist University School of Law, Dallas, Texas, 1970; admitted to the Texas Bar, 1971; law clerk for U.S. district judge for the Southern District of Texas, 1971-72; assistant district attorney, Harris County, Texas, 1972-76; commenced private practice in Houston, 1976; member: State Bar of Texas, Houston and American Bar Associations; member, St. Lukes United Methodist Church; married to former Ann Bowman of Houston, Texas; two children: Caroline and Emily; elected to the 98th Congress, November 2, 1982.

•ANTONY, EDWIN LE ROY, (1852-1913)- U. S. Representative, was born in Waynesboro, Burke County, Ga., January 5; moved with his parents to Texas in 1859 and settled in Brasoria County; moved to Milam County in 1867; attended the common schools, and was graduated from the University of Georgia at Athens in 1873; studied law; was admitted to the bar in 1874 and commenced practice in Cameron, Texas; prosecuting attorney of Milam County 1876, being also ex officio district attorney for his county; was appointed special judge during the illness of the regular district judge in 1886; member of the board of aldermen of Cameron 1890-1892; elected as a Democrat to the Fifty-second Congress to fill the vacancy caused by the resignation of Roger Q. Mills, and served from June 14, 1892, to March 3, 1893; unsuccessful candidate for renomination in 1892; resumed the practice of law in Cameron, Texas; died in Dallas, Texas, January 16.

•ARCHER, BILL, (1928-)- U. S. Representative, Republican, of Houston, Texas; was born in Houston, March 22; graduated from St. Thomas High School, salutatorian, 1945; attended Rice University, 1945-46; University of Texas, B.B.A., LL.B. (with honors), 1946-51; served in the U.S. Air Force, Korean conflict; captain, USAF Reserve; councilman and mayor pro tempore, city of Hunters Creek Village, 1955-62; elected to Texas House of Representatives, 1966; reelected, 1968; attorney and businessman; president, Uncle Johnny Mills, Inc., 1953-61;

member of Saint Anne's Catholic Church; member, Sigma Alpha Epsilon fraternity; chosen Houston S.A.E. Man of the Year; St. Thomas High School Alumnus Award; Houston B'nai B'rith "Man of the Year" Award; member, Phi Delta Phi legal fraternity; life member, Houston Livestock Show and Rodeo; N.F.I.B. "Guardian of Small Business" Award; N.A.B. "Watchdog of the Treasury" Award; National Alliance of Senior Citizens "Golden Age Hall of Fame" Award; president, Texas State Society of Washington, D.C., 1974-75; Spring Branch-Memorial Chamber of Commerce "Most Representative Citizen" Award; Brotherhood Award, National Conference of Christians and Jews; University of Texas 1981 Distinguished Alumnus Award; married; five children; elected to 92d Congress, November 3, 1970; reelected to each succeeding Congress; member, Committee on Ways and Means: ranking Republican, Subcommittee on Social Security; member, Subcommittee on Trade, official Congressional Trade Adviser; member, White House Commission on Regulatroy Reform, 1975-76; chairman, Republican Study Committee Task Force on Regulatory Reform, 1975-76; member, National Commission on Social Security Reform, 1982-83.

•AUSTIN, STEPHEN F. (1793-1836), early Texas leader, was born in Wythe County, Virginia, and was raised in Missouri by his parents, *Moses and Maria (Brown) Austin*. His father investigated the possibility of settling Spanish-controlled Texas in 1820. However, he died after a difficult trip. Young Stephen had completed studies at Transylvania University at Lexington, Kentucky, and was engaged in mining at Potosi, Missouri. When his father died, Austin had worked his way up to a position as director of the Bank of St. Louis, and had completed six years on the Missouri legislature. Afterwards, he moved to Arkansas territory, began a farm along the Red River, and took an appointment as a judge of the first judicial district (1820). In 1821, he became interested in completing what his father had started in Texas. At San Antonio that year, the Spanish officials granted him a claim to land for settlement by English speaking Americans. His first colony was on the west bank of the Brazos River near the present site of Washington in late 1921. Another group located on the Colorado River near present Columbia. The

Central Mexican government informed Austin that his land grants had not been cleared, however, and so he had to journey to Mexico City for final approval. He stayed there for a year, during which time the revolution took place. Austin consequently gained formal permission for his colonies, and also was given administrative power over the settlers until the Mexican government could be set up. The government continued to give Austin land for his efforts at bringing in immigrants, who were needed to accelerate the Texas economy. He framed a code of civil and criminal law, and organized an anti-Indian militia group among the colonists. By 1824, 300 families had settled Austin's land, and he brought in thousands more in the next seven years. The colonists and Austin began to prosper, but within a few years they grew hostile toward the Mexican government. Austin was against freeing slaves, and when the Coahila government abolished it in 1829, he worked out a plan to bring black workers into the colony as indentured servants, which didn't change their status significantly. The Austin colonists wished to form their own state under Mexican rule, but plans for a new constitution were refused by the Mexican government. When Austin went to the capital to argue their case, he was arrested as a revolutionary and jailed for a year without trial. When he was finally allowed to leave Mexico City in 1835, he found that many of the colonists' demands had been met. However, the colony was still a part of the state of Coahila, and a dispute over the location of a state capital resulted in what is now known as the Texas Revolution. While Austin was gone to the United States with a comission to learn the government's attitude on annexation, the Texas Declaration of Independence was signed. The Republic's first President, *Sam Houston,* appointed him Secretary of State, but he died of a fever at a convention in Columbia before he could fill out his term.

B

•BAILEY, JOSEPH WELDON, (1862-1929)- U. S. Representative and U. S. Senator, was born near Crystal Springs, Copiah County, Miss., October 6; attended the common schools; studied law; was admitted to the bar in 1883 and commenced practice in Hazlehurst, Miss; presidential elector on the Democratic ticket of Cleveland and Hendricks in 1884; moved to Gainesville, Texas, in 1885 and continued the practice of law; presidential elector on the Democratic ticket of Cleveland and Thurman in 1888; elected as a Democrat to the Fifty-second and to the four succeeding Congresses (March 4, 1891-March 3, 1901); was not a candidate for renomination in 1900; upon the organization of the Fifty-fifth Congress was the Democratic nominee for Speaker of the House of Representatives; elected to the United States Senate in 1901, reelected in 1907, and served from March 4, 1901, until January 3, 1913, when he resigned; resumed the practice of law in Washington, D. C.; subsequently, on March 3, 1921, moved to Dallas, Texas, and engaged in the practice of his profession; was an unsuccessful candidate for Governor of Texas in 1920; died in a courtroom in Sherman, Texas, on April 13.

•BAILEY, JOSEPH WELDON, JR., (1892-1943)- (son of the preceding)- U. S. Representative, was born in Gainesville, Cooke County, December 15; attended the public schools in Gainesville, Texas and Washington, D. C.; was graduated from Princeton University, Princeton, N. J., in 1915 and from the University of Virginia at Charlottesville in 1919; during the First World War served as a first lieutenant in the Three Hundred and Fourteenth Regiment of Field Artillery from August 15, 1917, to March 24, 1919; studied law; was admitted to the bar in 1920 and commenced practice in Fort Worth, Texas; moved to Dallas, Texas, the

11

same year and continued the practice of his profession; delegate to the Democratic State conventions from 1922 to 1934; elected as a Democrat to the Seventy-third Congress (March 4, 1933-January 3, 1935); was not a candidate for renomination in 1934, but was an unsuccessful candidate for the Democratic nomination for United States Senator; resumed the practice of law in Dallas, Texas; during World War II served as a captain in the Marine Corps from May 13, 1942, until his death in an Army hospital at Gainesville, Texas, July 17.

•BALL, THOMAS HENRY, (1869-1944)- U. S. Representative, was born in Huntsville, Walker County, January 14; attended private schools; was graduated from Austin College, Sherman, Texas, in 1876; studied law at the University of Virginia at Charlottesville; was admitted to the bar in 1886 and commenced practice in Huntsville, Texas; mayor of Huntsville 1887-1893; chairman of the Democratic executive committee of Walker County 1884-1896; delegate to all State conventions from 1886 to 1924, with three exceptions; delegate to the Democratic National Conventions in 1892, 1924, and 1928; elected as a Democrat to the Fifty-fifth and to the three succeeding Congresses and served from March 4, 1897, to November 16, 1903, when he resigned; resumed the practice of his profession; unsuccessful candidate for the Democratic gubernatorial nomination in 1914; general counsel for the State council of defense during the First World War; general counsel for the port commission of the Houston Harbor and Ship Channel from May 1922 to August 1931, when he retired; died in Houston, May 7.

•BARTLETT, STEVE, (1947-)- U. S. Representative, Republican, of Dallas, Texas; was born in Los Angeles, California on September 19; attended Lockhart Elementary School, Lockhart, Texas; graduated, Kimball High School, Dallas, Texas, 1966; B.A., University of Texas, Austin, Texas, 1971; businessman; member of city council, Dallas, Texas, 1977-81; member: Dental Health Programs Board, North Dallas

Chamber, Neighborhood Housing Services of Dallas, Birthright, Inc.; married to the former Gail Coke in 1969; three children: Allison, Courtney, and Brian; elected on November 2, 1982 to the 98th Congress.

•BASS, SAM (1851-1878), outlaw, was born in Mitchell, Indiana to *Daniel and Elizabeth Sheeks Bass*, farmers. His mother died in 1861, and his father died three years later, so he was left with an uncle. He disliked school and probably never learned to read, mostly joining the other town roughnecks in fun and games. When he was 18, he left home for St. Louis, and then traveled down the Mississippi. Eventually, he settled in Denton, Texas, where he held various jobs, including deputy sheriff. Until about 1875, he was a law-abiding citizen, but he became more interested in gambling and horse-betting than work. He and some cronies stole horses from the Choctaws and Cherokees of the region. Soon thereafter, he and a local cattleman, *Joel Collins* drove a large herd of cattle into Kansas and kept the proceeds for themselves, although many of the herd belonged to ranchers back in Texas. The two then moved on to the Black Hills of South Dakota, where they supported their drinking and gambling habits with stagecoach raids and other acts of frontier thievery. Collins and Bass took up train robbing when they moved to Nebraska, the most famous incident taking place in 1877 at Big Springs when they gathered over $65,000 worth of gold. Their success was short-lived, however, because Collins and an assistant were caught and killed on their escape. Bass was able to return to Denton, where he gathered a new gang of outlaws to help him rob trains in the Dallas-Fort Worth area. An informant was hired by the the Texas Rangers to ride with Bass and his men, and on July 19, 1878, the Rangers were waiting for him when he tried to rob a bank at Round Rock. Bass was mortally wounded in the gunfight that ensued, and died two days later, on his birthday.

•BEAN, ROY (1825-1903), judge and frontiersman, was known as "the Law West of the Pecos" in his heyday in Western Texas. He was born in Mason County, Kentucky, and performed odd jobs during his boyhood. He later tried gold mining in the West and then became a trader in Mexico. He moved to Texas in 1875 to try to make his fortune as a saloon keeper. First settling in San Antonio, he gained enough capital by 1882 to move to the lower Pecos River area and opened a series of saloons along the new railroad lines being built across that cattle country. He settled in the dusty village of Vinegaroon near the Rio Grande, and operated a successful saloon for workers at the railroad terminus there. The roughly 8,000 inhabitants soon regarded Bean as a sort of father figure and informally nominated him as their justice of the peace. Bean also acted as a coroner on a number of occasions. He held court at the bar of his saloon, and became well known for his unusual decisions and threatening gestures with his six gun. Once, he fined a corpse $40 for carrying illegal weapons. "The Law West of the Pecos" found that he could not hold a boxing match in the state of Texas, so in 1898 he coordinated a contest between heavyweight champion *Robert Fitzsimmons* and *Peter Maher* that took place near his settlement on a sandbar in the Rio Grande. Bean once fell in love with the English actress *Lillie Langtry*, and named his saloon for her: "The Jersey Lily." However, his town of Langtry was not named for the actress; in 1881, a civil engineer by that name surveyed the railroad site there. Bean died in that town.

•BECKWORTH, LINDLEY GARY, (1913-)- U. S. Representative, was born on a farm in the South Bouie community near Mabank, Kaufman County, Texas, June 30; attended the rural schools, Abilene Christian College, East Texas State Teachers College, Commerce, Texas, Sam Houston State Teachers College, Huntsville, Texas, and Southern Methodist University, Dallas, Texas; taught school in Upshur County, Texas, for three years; attended the law department of Baylor University, Waco, Texas, and the University of Texas at Austin; was admitted to the bar in 1937 and commenced practice in Gilmer, Texas; member of the State house of representatives 1936-1938; elected as a Democrat to the Seventy-sixth and to the six succeeding Congresses (January 3, 1939-January 3, 1953); was not a candidate for renomination in 1952, but was unsuccessful for the

Democratic nomination for United States Senator; resumed the practice of law in Longview, Texas; elected to the Eighty-fifth and to the four succeeding Congresses (January 3, 1957-January 3, 1967); unsuccessful candidate for renomination in 1966; judge, United States Custom Court, New York, N. Y., 1967-1968; resumed the practice of law.

•BEE, CARLOS, (1867-1932) (great-grandson of Thomas Bee)- U. S. Representative, was born in Saltillo, Mexico, July 8, where his parents had moved after the collapse of the Confederacy; returned with his parents to San Antonio, Texas, in 1874; attended the public schools and the Agricultural and Mechanical College; studied law while working as a railway mail clerk; was admitted to the bar in 1893 and commenced practice in San Antonio, Texas; United States commissioner for the western district of Texas in 1893; district attorney of the thirty-seventh judicial district 1898-1905; chairman of the Democratic State convention in 1904; delegate to the Democratic National Convention at St. Louis, Mo., in 1904 and at Denver, Colo., in 1908; served as a member of the city school board of San Antonio 1906-1908; president of the county school board of Bexar County, Texas, 1912-1914; member of the State senate 1915-1919; elected as a Democrat to the Sixty-sixth Congress (March 4, 1919-March 3, 1921); unsuccessful candidate for reelection in 1920 to the Sixty-seventh Congress; engaged in the practice of law in San Antonio, Texas, until his death there on April 20.

•BELL, CHARLES KEITH, (1853-1913) (nephew of Reese Bowen Brabson)- U. S. Representative, was born in Chattanooga, Tenn., April 18; attended the public schools and Sewanee (Tenn.) College; moved to Texas in 1871; studied law; was admitted to the bar in 1874 and commenced practice in Hamilton,Texas; prosecuting attorney of Hamilton County in 1876; district attorney 1880-1882; delegate to the Democratic National Convention at Chicago in 1884; member of the State senate 1884-1888; judge of the twenty-ninth judicial district of Texas 1888-1890; elected as a

Democrat to the Fifty-third and Fifty-fourth Congresses (March 4, 1893-March 3, 1897); was not a candidate for renomination in 1896; resumed the practice of law in Fort Worth, Texas; attorney general of Texas 1901-1904; again resumed the practice of law in Fort Worth, where he died April 21.

•BELL, JOHN JUNIOR, (1910-1963)- U. S. Representative, was born in Cuero, De Witt County, May 15; attended the public schools; was graduated from the University of Texas at Austin in 1932 and from its law school in 1936; was admitted to the bar in 1936 and commenced the practice of law in Cuero, Texas; served in the State house of representatives 1937-1947; president of a company operating compresses in Victoria, Shiner, Cuero, and Taft, Texas; during World War II served as a private in the United States Army from May 1944 to March 1945; member of the State senate 1947-1954; delegate to the Democratic National Conventions in 1948 and 1952; elected as a Democrat to the Eighty-fourth Congress (January 3, 1955-January 3, 1957); unsuccessful candidate for renomination in 1956; lawyer, rancher, and farmer; was a resident of Cuero, Texas, until his death January 24.

•BELL, PETER H. (1812-98), third governor of Texas (1849-53), was a native of Culpepper, Virginia and the son of *Colonel James and Amelia Hansborough Bell.* He studied in his home state and Maryland taking some college courses before becoming a merchant in Petersburg, Virginia in the early 1830s. In 1836, however, he enlisted under *General Houston* to fight in the Texas Revolution, and helped in the battle of San Jacinto. He was so popular that he was made inspector-general of the army of Texas soon afterwards. In 1845 he was made captain of the Texas Rangers and during the Mexican War served as a colonel of volunteers under *General Zachary Taylor.* A Democrat, Bell was elected governor over the incumbent. He had to deal with the Indian attacks on the ever-increasing German and French settlers in Texas at that time. In 1850, during his first administration, Bell's

commission on boundaries established the line between Mexico
and Texas from the Rio Grande, At the intersection of the thirty-
second degree of north latitude, to the Pacific Ocean. Bell was
reelected in 1851, but resigned before his term was over to take a
seat in Congress. Bell's major success was in gaining $10 million
in compensation from the federal government for the lost lands in
the Santa Fe, or western region of what was once Texas. This is
known as the Compromise of 1850. In Congress, he represented
the western district of Texas, fighting to keep those boundaries
intact. He retired after his second term in 1857, married *Ella
Eaton* of North Carolina, and maintained a plantation there. He
was a colonel on the Confederate side during the Civil War. The
Texas government granted him land and a pension for his services in 1891, but he remained at Littleton, North Carolina until
his death.

•BENTSEN, LLOYD MILLARD, JR., (1921-)- U. S. Representative and U. S. Senator, was born in Mission, Hidalgo County,
February 11; attended the public schools; was graduated from
the law school of the University of Texas at Austin in 1942 and was
admitted to the bar the same year; during World War II enlisted
as a private in the United States Army in April 1942 and served
until discharged as a major in July 1945; commenced the practice of law in McAllen, Texas, in 1945; elected county judge of
Hidalgo County, Texas, in 1946 and served until March 1948;
elected as a Democrat on November 2, 1948, to the Eighty-first
Congress, and, at a special election on December 4, 1948, to fill
the vacancy in the Eightieth Congress caused by the death of
Milton H. West; reelected to the Eighty-second and Eighty-third
Congresses and served from December 4, 1948, to January 3,
1955; was not a candidate for renomination in 1954; founded Con-
solidated American Life Insurance Co., and in 1958 merged with
Lincoln Liberty Life Insurance Co., and served as president of
Lincoln Consolidate, Inc., with headquarters in Houston, Texas;
member, board of directors: Houston Chamber of Commerce,
Houston Society of Performing Arts, and the United Fund of
Houston, Texas; elected as a Democrat on November 3, 1970, to
the United States Senate for the six-year term commencing
January 3, 1971.

•BENTSEN, LLOYD MILLARD (1921-), U.S. Senator, was born in Mission, Texas on February 11, 1921. He graduated from the University of Texas in 1942 with an LL.B. degree and enlisted in the U.S. Army the same year. During World War II he served as a squadron commander in the Army Air Corps, flew 50 missions over Europe and attained the rank of colonel. He was awarded the Distinguished Flying Cross and the Air Medal with three oak leaf clusters. In 1943 he married Beryl Ann Longino of Lufkin, Texas. They have three children: Lloyd III, Lan and Tina.

In 1946 Bentsen was elected county judge of Hidalgo County, Texas. He served one term. In December of 1948 he was elected to the 80th U.S. Congress in a special election. He was reelected for the three subsequent terms before declining to seek reelection in 1954. In 1955 he moved to Houston to enter business and became the president of Lincoln Consolidated, a financial holding institution. He also served on the board of directors of a number of major corporations. He ran for the Senate in 1970 and was elected for the six year term. He was reelected in the following term and again in 1982. In the Senate he has served as chairman of the Democratic Senatorial Campaign Committee, as well as on the Finance, Environment and Public Works, Intelligence, Joint Economic, and Joint Tax Committees.

•BIG TREE (1847-1927), Kiowa chief, also known as Ado-ette, rose to prominence as a war chief during the late 1860s. His active role in the Texas raiding parties of 1868 earned him recognition as a war chief before he was 25 years old. He maintained a leadership role despite incarceration in a Texas prison and conversion to Christianity.

In May 1871, a group of Kiowa warriors, led by Chiefs *Satanta, Setangya,* and Big Tree, killed seven men and confiscated 41 mules in a raid in Texas. *Satanta* boasted of this raid to the Indian agent at Fort Sill, Oklahoma, and to *Gen. William T. Sherman,* naming *Setangya* and Big Tree as co-leaders. *Sherman* promptly arrested the three chiefs and *Setangya* was killed when he resisted being transported in chains to Texas for trial. The other two chiefs were held at Fort Richardson, Texas, and were then sent to stand trial in nearby Jacksboro, Texas, where they were convicted of murder by a cowboy jury on July 5, 1871, and sentenced to death by hanging.

Their death sentences were commuted to life imprisonment in August 1871 by the Texas governor following the intervention of the Indian agent, *Lawrie Tatum*, and his fellow Quakers.

Big Tree and *Satanta* were escorted from prison to St. Louis, Missouri, in September 1872 to meet with a Kiowa delegation going to Washington, D.C. The St. Louis meeting was a tribal condition to be met before the delegates went to Washington. The federal authorities agreed because they hoped to impress the Kiowa delegates with U.S. power during their visit to the nation's capital.

After two years of confinement in the Huntsville, Texas, penitentiary, Big Tree and *Satanta* were removed to the guardhouse at Fort Sill in August 1873, and in October they were released on parole after promising that the tribe would continue their good conduct. The two chiefs were accused of participating in several outbreaks in 1874, but their agent declared their innocence.

Big Tree and *Satanta* were present during a fight at the Anadarko Agency in August 1874. Fearful of being accused of instigating the fight, they fled west to the Antelope Hills. Having second thoughts, Big Tree surrendered on September 29, 1874, at the Cheyenne and Arapaho Agency at Darlington, Texas. *Satanta* came in on October 4, and both chiefs were returned to Fort Sill by military authorities. *Satanta's* parole was revoked and he was recommitted to the Texas State Penitentiary where, in 1878, he committed suicide. Big Tree was allowed to remain free on parole.

Big Tree was the Kiowa delegate to the International Council of Tribes in 1888 at Fort Gibson, which was called by the Five Civilized Tribes to oppose the opening of Indian territory (now Oklahoma). He later opposed the opening of the Kiowa Reservation pursuant to the Jerome Agreement of October 6, 1892, on the grounds that tribal consent had not been obtained.

He had his band settle in the area of Rainy Mountain, Oklahoma, where he lived until his death. He apparently became interested in Christianity in 1893 and in 1897 joined the Rainy Mountain Baptist Church where he was eventually elected a deacon.

•BING, ROBERT H. (1914-), educator and mathematician, was born in Oakwood, Texas on October 20, 1914. He was educated at the Southwest Texas State Teachers College, and the University of Texas, where he received in Master's and a Doctorate in Science Education. Dr. Bing has taught at the University of Texas, University of Wisconsin, and the University of Virginia. He is a former president of the Mathematical Association of America, and a member of American Mathematical Society. Dr. Bing has served as math division chairman of the National Academy of Sciences, and a member of the Institute of Advanced Study. He is the author of numerous research papers published in mathematical journals. He is married and has four children.

•BLACK, EUGENE, (1879-)- U. S. Representative, was born near Blossom, Lamar County, July 2; attended the public schools of Blossom; taught school in Lamar County 1898-1900; employed in the post office at Blossom; was graduated from the law department of Cumberland University, Lebanon, Tenn., in 1905; was admitted to the bar the same year and commenced practice in Clarksville, Red River County, Texas; was also engaged in the wholesale grocery business; elected as a Democrat to the Sixty-fourth and to the six succeeding Congresses (March 4, 1915-March 3, 1929); unsuccessful candidate for renomination in 1928; appointed by President Hoover to the United States Board of Tax Appeals (now the Tax Court of the United States) in November 1929 to fill an unexpired term; reappointed in 1932 and again in 1944 by President Franklin D. Roosevelt for a term of twelve years and served until his retirement November 30, 1953; recalled December 1, 1953, to perform further judicial service with Tax Court of the United States; is a resident of Washington, D. C.

•BLAKLEY, WILLIAM ARVIS, (1898-1961)- U. S. Senator, was born in Miami Station, Saline County, Mo., November 17; moved with his parents to Arapaho, Custer County, Okla., and graduated from Arapaho High School; during the First World War served in the United States Army; attorney and certified public accountant in Dallas, Texas, since 1924; has interests in oil fields, ranching, and real estate; admitted to the bar on June 14, 1933, and commenced practice in Dallas, Texas; appointed as a Democrat by Gov. Allan Shivers to the United States Senate to fill the vacancy caused by the resignation of Price Daniel and served from January 15, 1957, to April 28, 1957; declined to be a candidate for election to the vacancy; unsuccessful candidate for the Democratic nomination for a full term to the United States Senate in 1958; appointed to the United States Senate to fill the vacancy caused by the resignation of Lyndon B. Johnson and served from January 3, 1961, to June 14.

•BLANTON, THOMAS LINDSAY, (1872-1957)- U. S. Representative, was born in Houston, Harris County, October 25; educated in the public schools; was graduated from the law department of the University of Texas at Austin in 1897, with three years in the academic department; was admitted to the bar in 1897 and commenced practice in Cleburne, Texas; moved to Albany, Texas, and continued the practice of law until 1908, when he was elected judge of the forty-second judicial district of Texas; reelectd in 1912 and served in that capacity from 1908 until elected to Congress; elected as a Democrat to the Sixty-fifth and to the five succeeding Congresses (March 4, 1917-March 3, 1929); was not a candidate for renomination in 1928, but was an unsuccessful candidate for nomination to the United States Senate; subsequently elected on May 20 1930, to the Seventy-first Congress to fill the vacancy caused by the death of Robert Q. Lee; reelected to the Seventy-second, Seventy-third, and Seventy-fourth Congresses and served from May 20, 1930, to January 3, 1937; unsuccessful candidate for renomination in 1936; engaged in the practice of law in Washington, D. C., in 1937 and 1938; returned to Albany, Texas, in 1938, and continued practicing law; also engaged in the raising of Hereford cattle; died in Albany, Texas, August 11.

•BORDEN, GAIL (1801-1874), inventor and industrialist, was the oldest son of *Gail and Philadelphia (Wheeler) Borden* of Norwich, New York. He was a boy of 13 when the family moved west to Kentucky and then to Indiana. A sickly adolescent, he was sent to Mississippi in 1822 because of its milder climate. There, he taught school and learned surveying. However, the weather wasn't as beneficial as he had hoped, and in 1829 he moved to Austin's new colony with his young wife. He joined the colonists' movement to form a separate state, attending the 1833 convention which framed a state constitution. He also drew the first topographical map of Texas, and headed the San Felipe land office until the Mexican Revolution. Then he began publishing the "Telegraph and Texas Land Register" with his brother *Thomas*. The new Republic assigned Borden to survey and plan the city of Galveston in 1839, and he served as an agent for the Galveston City Company until 1851. Borden was crushed by the deaths of his wife and two of his children and resolved to do something to improve the health of pioneers of the West. He developed a new form of dried meat, which was used by Arctic explorers and honored at the 1851 British Exposition. Army suppliers forced him out of business within two years, however, and he returned to New York, bankrupt, in 1853. Borden then concentrated on the product he has become famous for, condensed milk. His first company began beef broth, for which he opened a plant in Colorado County, Texas, as well as reducing coffee, tea, cocoa and fruit juice to one-seventh of their original volumes. The public purchased these early convenience foods with a relish. Borden, whose main company offices were in New York, Jersey City and Chicago, moved back to Texas in 1861 to supervise his holding in Colorado County. Evaporated milk became even more popular after the Civil War, since the Union Troops found it convenient and healthful. Borden died at his company town, Borden. A county in West Texas, as well at its county seat, Gail, were named in his honor.

•BOWIE, JAMES (1796-1836), adventurer and soldier, is best known for his heroism at the Alamo. He was born in Burke County, Georgia, the son of *J. Rezin* and *Alvina Jones Bowie*. The family moved to Louisiana in 1802, where he enjoyed such activities as bear-fighting, alligator-riding and taming wild horses. Some sources also indicate that he and two of his brothers began to trade slaves illegally with the pirate *Lafitte* along the Louisiana and Texas coastlines. It has been substantiated, however, that he made his legal living as a bargeman and logger. In 1819, he joined an unsuccessful revolutionary expedition into Texas. In 1827, he supposedly got into a fight on the banks of the Mississippi near Natchez in which he was badly wounded by a bullet, but was able to kill his assailant with a knife. In the meantime, his brothers had been selling fraudulent land grants in Arkansas. Perhaps to escape his past, he moved to Texas in 1828, settling in Mexican-ruled San Antonio. He tried prospecting for a lost mine in the San Saba region, and two years later was made a Mexican citizen, which allowed him to acquire large tracts of land at cheap rates. He married *Maria de Veramendi*, daughter of the vice-governor at San Antonio in 1831, which gained him favor. Since he never found the lost mine of San Saba, Bowie explored the Texas-Louisiana-Mississippi region, speculated on land and became more and more interested in resistance of the Mexican government. He was a captain in the 1832 fight in Nacogdoches, and was chosen as a member of the first committee of safety at Mina (now Bastrop) in 1835. As the revolution broke out, Bowie was in his element as a colonel, becoming one of the main factors forcing the retreat of the Mexican Army in late 1835. The army returned to San Antonio in early 1836, however, and Bowie found himself in the middle of the fray, along with *Colonel William Travis* and about 150 men. The soldiers were forced to retreat across the river and defend themselves at the abandoned Alamo mission. Bowie fought as best he could, but fell ill, and was killed by the Mexicans when they finally captured the Alamo on March 6.

Bowie is often attributed as the inventor of the Bowie Knife. However, more evidence shows that it was his brother, *Rezin*, who designed the classic Western knife. James Bowie used it successfully in his 1827 fight along the Mississippi.

•BOX, JOHN CALVIN, (1871-1941)- U. S. Representative, was born near Crockett, Houston County, March 28; attended the country schools, and Alexander Collegiate Institute (later Lon Morris College), Kilgore, Texas; studied law; was admitted to the bar in 1893 and commenced practice in Lufkin, Texas; moved to Jacksonville, Cherokee County, Texas, in 1897 and continued the practice of his profession; also a licensed Methodist minister; judge of the Cherokee County Court 1898-1901; mayor of Jacksonville 1902-1905; member of the Democratic State committee 1908-1910; member of the board of education and served as chairman 1913-1918; elected as a Democrat to the Sixty-sixth and to the five succeeding Congresses (March 4, 1919-March 3, 1931); unsuccessful candidate for renomination in 1930; reengaged in the practice of law in Jacksonville, Texas, until his death there May 17.

•BRIGGS, CLAY STONE, (1876-1933)- U. S. Representative, was born in Galveston, January, 8; attended private and public schools, the University of Texas at Austin, and Harvard University, Cambridge, Mass.; was graduated from the law department of Yale University, New Haven, Conn., in 1899; was admitted to the bar the same year and commenced the practice of law in Galveston, Texas; member of the State house of representatives 1906-1908; served as judge of the tenth judicial district of Texas from June 15, 1909, until February 1, 1919, when he resigned, having been elected to Congress; elected as a Democrat to the Sixty-sixth and to the seven succeeding Congresses and served from March 4, 1919, until his death in Washington; D. C., April 29; interment in Oakwood Cemetery, Syracuse, N.Y.

•BRISCOE, DOLPH (1923-), fortieth governor of Texas (1973-79), was born in Uvalde, Texas, the son of *Dolph Sr., and Georgie Briscoe* (his mother was his father's cousin and had the same last name). He attended public school in town, and then studied at the University of Texas (A.B., 1942). He was an army officer during the World War, and then returned to his home area to work on the family ranch. He was voted Outstanding Conservation Rancher of Texas in 1958. He was soon one of the wealthiest ranchers in South Texas, and represented his district in the state legislature for many years (1949-57). He was an active Democrat, but didn't hold any more elected office until he ran against the shamefaced *Governor Smith* in 1972. However, he defeated the Republican candidate by only 100,000 votes, or 47 percent of the total vote. Governor Briscoe was an innocuous governor, a needed rest after the turmoil of Smith's term. He was able to befriend minority groups and labor leaders as well as the rich ranchers and oil company executives in Texas. He brought no new taxes, and supported strong law enforcement, school finances, but did not support the movement for a constitutional convention at that time. He was reelected in 1974, this time for a four-year term under the new Constitution. He was not the Democratic candidate in the next election, however. Briscoe subsequently returned to his ranch, where he now resides.

•**BRITAIN, RADIE** (1903-), composer, was born on March 17, 1903 in Amarillo, Texas. Ms Radie received her education at the University of Chicago, and the American Conservatory in Chicago. After graduation she made her musical debut in Munich, Germany in 1925 while pursuing advanced study. Ms. Britian continued her training in piano and won a gold medal in organ composition. Upon returning to American she spent two seasons in the McDowell Artistic Colony where *Southern Symphone* and *Light* were composed. Her compositions have been played by America's leading symphony orchestras. Among the prizes awarded to her include: International Heroic Poem for Orchestra, Julliard Prize, and First National Prize for *Suite for Strings*. Ms Bing is married and has one child.

•**BROOCKS, MOSES LYCURGUS,** (1864-1908)- U. S. Representative, was born near San Augustine, San Augustine County, November 1; attended the common schools; was graduated from the law department of the University of Texas at Austin in 1891 and commenced practice at San Augustine; member of the State house of representatives in 1892; moved to Beaumont, Jefferson County, Texas; elected district attorney of the first judicial district of Texas in 1896 and served one term; elected as a Democrat to the Fifty-ninth Congress (March 4, 1905-March 3, 1907); resumed the practice of law in San Augustine, Texas and died there May 27.

•BROOKS, JACK BASCOM, (1922-)• U. S. Representative, was born in Crowley, Acadia Parish, La., December 18; moved with his family to Beaumont, Texas, in 1927; attended public schools and Lamar Junior College, Beaumont, Texas, 1939-1941; University of Texas at Austin, B. J., 1943; enlisted as a private in the United States Marine Corps November 7, 1942, serving overseas twenty-three and one-half months on Guadalcanal, Guam, Okinawa, and in North China, and discharged as a first lieutenant April 23, 1946; colonel in the United States Marine Corps Reserve; member of State house of representatives 1946-1950; graduated from the law school of the University of Texas in 1949; was admitted to the bar the same year and commenced the practice of law in Beaumont, Texas; owns and operates a farm; elected as a Democrat to the Eighty-third and to the eight succeeding Congresses (January 3, 1953-January 3, 1971). Reelected to the Ninety-second Congress.

•BRYAN, GUY MORRISON, (1821-1901)- U. S. Representative, was born in Herculaneum, Jefferson County, Mo., January 12; moved to the Mexican State of Texas in 1831 with his parents, who settled near San Felipe; attended private schools; joined the Texas Army at San Jacinto in 1836 and fought for the cause of the Republic; was graduated from Kenyon College, Gambier, Ohio, in 1842; studied law, but never practiced; engaged in planting; served as a private in the Brazoria company, under the command of Captain Ballowe, during the Mexican War with the Texas Volunteers on the eastern bank of the Rio Grande; member of the State house of representatives 1847-1853; served in the State senate 1853-1857; delegate to the Democratic National Convention at Cincinnati in 1856; chairman of the Texas delegation in the Democratic National Convention at Baltimore in 1860; elected as a Democrat to the Thirty-fifth Congress (March 4, 1857-March 3, 1859); was not a candidate for renomination in 1858; during the Civil War served as volunteer aide-de-camp on the staff of General Herbert and afterwards as assistant adjutant general, with the rank of major, of the trans-Mississippi Department; established a cotton bureau in Houston, Texas, in order to escape the blockade along the Gulf; moved to Galveston, Texas, in 1872; again a member of the State house of representatives in 1873, 1879, and 1887-1891, and served as speaker in 1873; moved to Quintana, Texas, in 1890 and to Austin, Travis County, Texas, in 1898; elected president of the Texas Veterans Association in 1892 and served until his death in Austin, Texas, June 4.

•BRYANT, JOHN WILEY, (1947-)- U. S. Representative, Democrat, of Dallas, Texas; was born in Lake Jackson on February 22; graduated Brazosport High School, 1965; graduated, Southern Methodist University with a B.A. degree in 1969; Southern Methodist University School of Law, 1972; admitted to the bar in 1972; partner in law firm of Stanord & Bryant; served as chief counsel to the Texas Senate subcommittee on consumer affairs, 1973; elected to Texas House of Representatives in a special election, January 24, 1974; reelected in general election, 1974; reelected in 1976, served as chairman of House study group; reelected in 1978, served second term as chairman of house study group; reelected in 1980; member: White Rock United Methodist Church, Old Scyene Historical Society, Historical Preservation Society of Dallas, Dallas Bar Association, Mesquite Chamber of Commerce; board member of Deaf Action Center of Dallas; lifetime member of Lions Club Eye Bank; married to the former Janet Watts; three children: Amy, John, Jr., and Jordan; elected to the 98th Congress, November 2, 1982.

•BUCHANAN, JAMES PAUL, (1867-1937) (cousin of Edward William Pou)- U. S. Representative, was born in Midway, Orangeburg County, S. C., April 30; moved to Texas in 1867 with his parents, who settled near Chapel Hill, Washington County; attended the district school; was graduated from the law department of the University of Texas at Austin in 1889; was admitted to the bar and commenced practice in Brenham, Washington County, Texas; justice of the peace of Washington County 1889-1892; prosecuting attorney 1892-1899; district attorney for the twenty-first judicial district of Texas 1899-1906; served as a member of the State house of representatives 1906-1913; elected as a Democrat to the Sixty-third Congress to fill the vacancy caused by the resignation of Albert Sidney Burleson; reelected to the Sixth-fourth and to the eleven succeeding Congresses and served from April 5, 1913, until his death in Washington, D. C., February 22.

•BUCHHOLZ, DONALD ALDEN (1929-), CPA and stockbroker, was born on March 10, 1929 in LaPorte, Texas. After graduating from North Texas University with a B.A. in Business Administation Mr. Buchholz served in the U.S. Air Force 1946-49, before working in various accounting positions in the 1950's. During the 1960's he was involved in stockbrokerage, banking, and real estate. He served on the boards of a variety of corporations, and was a member of the Board of Governors of the New York Stock Exchange 1969-71. He is married and has one child.

•BURGESS, GEORGE FARMER, (1861-1919)- U. S. Representative, born in Wharton, Wharton County, September 21; attended the common schools; moved with his mother to Fayette County in 1880 and engaged in agricultural pursuits near Flatonia; was later employed as a clerk in a country store; studied law; was admitted to the bar in 1882 and commenced practice in La Grange, Texas; moved to Gonzales in 1884; prosecuting attorney of Gonzales County from 1886 to 1889, when he resigned; presidential elector on the Democratic ticket of Cleveland and Stevenson in 1892; elected as a Democrat to the Fifty-seventh and to the seven succeeding Congresses (March 4, 1901-March 3, 1917); unsuccessful candidate for the Democratic nomination of United States Senator in 1916; resumed the practice of law at Gonzales, Texas, where he died December 31.

•BURKE, ROBERT EMMET, (1847-1901)- U. S. Representative, was born near Dadeville, Tallapoosa County, Ala., August 1; attended the public schools of his native city; volunteered as a private in Company D, Tenth Georgia Cavalry, Confederate Army, at the age of sixteen and served throughout the Civil War; moved to Jefferson, Texas, in 1866; studied law; was admitted to the bar in November 1870f and commenced practice in Dallas, Texas in 1871; judge of Dallas County 1878-1888; judge of the fourteenth judicial district of Texas 1888-1896; elected as a Democrat to the Fifty-fifth, Fifty-sixth, and Fifty-seventh Congresses and served from March 4, 1897, until his death in Dallas, Texas, June 5.

•BURLESON, ALBERT SIDNEY, (1863-1937)- U. S. Representative, was born in San Marcos, Hays County, Texas, June 7; attended the public schools and Coronal Institute, San Marcos, Texas, and the Agricultural and Mechanical College, College Station, Texas; was graduated from Baylor University, Waco, Texas, in 1881 and from the law department of the University of Texas at Austin in 1884: was admitted to the bar in 1884 and commenced practice in Austin, Travis County, Texas, in 1885; assistant city attorney of Austin 1885-1890; served as district attorney of the twenty-sixth judicial district 1891-1898; elected as a Democrat to the Fifty-sixth and to the seven succeeding Congresses and served from March 4, 1899, until March 6, 1913, when he resigned to accept a Cabinet portfolio; appointed Postmaster General in the Cabinet of President Wilson and served from March 7, 1913, to March 4, 1921, when he retired from public life; chairman of the United States Telegraph and Telephone Administration in 1918; chairman of the United States Commission to the International Wire Communication Conference in 1920;

returned to Austin, Texas, and engaged in banking; also interested in agricultural pursuits and the raising of livestock; died in Austin, Texas, November 24.

•BURLESON, EDWARD (1798-1851), soldier and Indian-fighter, was born near Asheville in North Carolina, but moved to Kentucky when he was still a small boy. Along the way west, his grandfather, *Aaron Burleson*, was killed by Indians. Thereafter, the boy was raised to hate the red man. At the age of 15, he killed the leader of a band of Indians, and he was with *General Andrew Jackson* at the Battle of Horseshoe Bend in Alabama, where the Creek nation was defeated. He lived in Missouri and Tennessee for the next few years, and in 1831 settled with his family on the Colorado River, near Bastrop, Texas. He soon became a lieutenant colonel of the militia for the area because of his talents at killing Indians. Burleson also became interested in the cause of Texas independence, and in 1835 he led a battalion at the Battle of Mission Concepcion. Later, he succeeded *Stephen Austin* as commander of the Texas forces, and directed the attack on San Antonio when *General Cos* and his men were captured in late 1835. The following April, he joined the forces led by *General Houston* at the Battle of San Antonio, leading a regiment to victory. He was a member of the first Texas congress, and elected vice president of the Texas Republic in 1841. During that time, he was also sent on Indian fighting missions by the Republic government. The Cherokees were forced out of Texas as a result of one of his men's raids. He served in the war with Mexico and in 1848 was elected a member of the state senate. When he died at Austin, Texas, he was president of that body. He was the first person buried in the now-famous state cemetery.

•BURLESON, OMAR, (1906-)- U. S. Representative, Democrat, of Anson, Texas; was born March 19; son of J. M. and Betty Burleson; wife, Ruth; lawyer; county attorney and county judge of Jones County; special agent of FBI; 3 years in the United States Navy, World War II; elected to the 80th and succeeding Congresses.

•BUSH, GEORGE (HERBERT WALKER) (1924-), Vice-President of the United States, was born in Milton, Massachusetts on June 12, 1924, the son of Prescott Sheldon Bush and Dorothy Walker Bush. George grew up with his sister and three brothers in affluent Greenwich, Connecticut. He attended Greenwich Country Day School and later entered Phillips Academy in Andover, Massachusetts. He graduated in 1942 and enlisted in the U.S. Navy Reserve. He was commissioned an ensign, and became a member of the Torpedo Bomber Squadron on the light-aircraft carrier *San Jacinto* in late 1943 where he saw action in the Pacific. He returned home in late 1944 and was married a few weeks later to Barbara Pierce. After his release from active duty, he entered Yale University and graduated with a degree in economics three years later.

Upon graduation he went to work for an oilfield supply company in Texas, and later California. Returning to Texas in 1950, he and John Overby Bush formed the Bush-Overby Company, which dealt in oil and gas properties. He continued to work in the oil industry until the early 1960's. In 1964, Bush, an active Republican, ran for U.S. Senate and captured 62 percent of the vote in the first runoff that Texas Republicans had ever held. He failed in his bid for a second term, however, falling victim to the Lyndon Johnson landslide. In 1966, he tried again for office, this time running for the House of Representatives for Texas' Seventh Congressional district. He won over Democrat Frank Briscoe. Two years later, he was reelected without opposition.

In Congress, Bush served on the Ways and Means Committee and pursued a generally conservative course. In 1970, he tried once again for a seat in the Senate. But in spite of heavy campaigning and support from Richard Nixon's secret campaign fund, he lost the election. He also lost his "safe" House seat because of the campaign. In December of 1970 in recognition of his efforts, Nixon named Bush as Permanent Representative of the United States to the United Nations. Bush served in this position until 1973 when Nixon named him chairman of the Republican National Committee. The first pieces of the Watergate Scandal were beginning to surface. By the summer of 1974 the White House tape recordings which had been turned over to the Supreme Court made it clear that Nixon had tried to obstruct the FBI's investigation of the affair. Bush gave Nixon a letter on August 7 asking him to step down, and the next day Nixon announced his resignation.

Gerald Ford, on assuming the Presidency, offered Bush his choice of positions. Bush chose to become chief of the United States Liaison Office in the People's Republic of China. He arrived in Peking in October 1974 and served there until December of 1975 when he was asked by the President to head the Central Intelligence Agency. He remained in that position until 1976 when the Democrats took over the White House.

Convinced that the Carter Administration was "just plain incompetent", Bush began campaigning for the presidency in 1980. When Ronald Reagan won the Republican party nomination, Bush was named as the vice-presidential running mate. They won in a landslide election against Jimmy Carter, an event that signalled a new conservatism in the country. Their first term in office was characterized by "Reagonomics", an economic policy that included widespread spending cuts, tax cuts and an increase in defense spending. Reagan and Bush won a second term in office in 1984 in a race against Walter Mondale and Geraldine Ferraro, the first woman vice-presidential candidate for a major party. During the campaign, Bush debated Ferraro on national television.

Bush is the father of five children: George, Jeb, Neil, Marvin and Dorothy.

C

•CABELL, EARLE, (1906-)- U. S. Representative, Democrat, of Dallas, Texas; was born on a farm south of the Trinity River in Dallas County, October 27; a son and grandson of former mayors of the city of Dallas; graduated from North Dallas High School in 1925; attended Texas A. & M. and Southern Methodist University; with two brothers organized in 1932 Cabell's Inc. (dairies and drive-in food stores) and served as secretary-treasurer, executive vice president, president, and chairman of the board; married the former Elizabeth Holder of Little Rock, Ark., in 1932; two children, Elizabeth Lee (Mrs. William Pulley) and Earle, Jr.; member and officer of various professional, civic, and philanthropic organizations; formerly director and member of executive committee of Grand Avenue Bank & Trust Co., Dallas, Texas; member of Dallas Country Club, Dallas Athletic Club, McKinney Club Lake, and City Club; mayor of Dallas from May 1, 1961, until his resignation February 3, 1964, to be candidate for Congress; elected to the 89th Congress November 3, 1964; reelected to the 90th Congress November 8, 1966; reelected to the 91st Congress November 5, 1968; reelected to the 92d Congress November 3, 1970.

•CABEZA DE VACA, ALVAR NUNEZ (1490?-1556?), explorer, is credited as being the first European to explore the Texas region. He was born at Jerez de la Frontera, Spain, son of *Francisco de Vera and Teresa Cabeza de Vaca* and descendant on both sides of distinguised Spanish families. On the maternal side he was descended from *Martino Alhaja*, a shepherd, who was given a patent of nobility by *King Sancho* of Navarre because of his service in guiding the Christian army through a mountain pass, enabling it to reach the rear of the Moorish army and thus win the

33

decisive battle of Las Navas de Tolosa in 1212. Because he mark-
ed the entrance to the pass with a cow's skull *Martino* became
known as *Cabeza de Vaca* (cow's head). In accordance with a
common Spanish custom the explorer took the name of his
mother's family. Little is known of his early life except that as a
young man he saw considerable military service. In February
1527 he was appointed treasurer, or collector of royal revenue,
with an expedition recruited to occupy the mainland of America
under the command of *Panfilo de Narvaez.* The expedition, consisting of five caravels carrying 600 men, sailed from San Lucar,
Spain, June 17, 1527, reached Santo Domingo early in August and
arrived at Santiago, Cuba, about two months later. Over 100 of
the expeditionaries deserted during the six weeks' sojourn in Santo Domingo and 60 more perished in a hurricane off the coast of
Cuba, which also destroyed several of their ships. As a result of
this disaster the expedition was forced to remain in Cuba until
late in February 1528, when, with a new ship purchased in
Trinidad, they set sail for Florida, landing 40 days later in Tampa
bay, then known as Espiritu Santo. The entire territory was
declared the lawful possession of the king of Spain. Subsequently,
against the advice of de Vaca, *Narvaez* decided on an advance
inland in search of gold, and on May 1 the expedition, consisting
of 300 men and 40 horses, began the northward march along the
western coast of Florida, reaching a point on the shores of Mic-
cosukee lake in Jefferson County, near the present boundary of
Georgia. Compelled to retreat by lack of food supplies and
damaging warfare with the Indians, the expedition struck south
and west, finally arriving at a place which they called Aute and
which seems to have been near the present site of St. Marks,
Wakulla County, Florida. Still harassed by Indians, the surviving
members of the expedition built crude rafts on which they embarked on September 22. All of them except Cabeza de Vaca and
three others were either lost at sea or died of hardship or at the
hands of hostile Indians on coasts where their craft had
foundered. De Vaca passed five years in slavery among various
tribes. Escaping finally with his three companions, he made his
way westward and after much hardship reached the western
coast of Mexico on the Gulf of California. Thus he was one of the
first four men to cross the North American continent. In his
travels he covered much of the territory which is now the central

states, southern United States and northern Mexico. He returned to Spain in 1537 to urge on the *Emperor Charles V* a more humane treatment of the natives of America. A detailed narrative of his North American travels was published at Amora in 1542 under the title of "La Relacion que Dio Alvar Nunez Cabeca de Vaca de lo Acaescido en las Indias en la Armada donde Yua por Gubernador Paphilo de Narbaez, desde el ano de Veynte y Siete hasta el Ano de Treynta y Seys..." This work passed through several editions and translated into English, French and German under various titles. In 1540 de Vaca was appointed governor of La Plata. His considerate treatment of the Indians aroused the resentment of his fellow Spaniards, and he was finally arrested and sent back to Spain, where he was tried and convicted on a charge of malfeasance and sentenced to banishment. Pardoned in 1552, he was appointed a judge of the high court of Seville and served in this office until his death, which occurred, probably in Seville, about 1556.

•CALLAWAY, OSCAR, (1872-1947)- U. S. Representative, was born i Harmony Hill (Nip-and-Tuck), Rusk County, Texas, October 2; moved with his parents to Commanche County in 1876; attended the public schools, and was graduated from the Comanche High School in 1894; taught school 1894-1897; attended the University of Texas at Austin 1897-1899, and was graduated from the law department of that university in 1900; was admitted to the bar the same year and commenced practice in Comanche, Texas; prosecuting attorney of Comanche County 1900-1902; delegate to Democratic State conventions in 1896, 1898, 1900-1916, and 1920-1926; elected as a Democrat to the Sixty-second, Sixty-third, and Sixty-fourth Congresses (March 4, 1911-March 3, 1917); unsuccessful candidate for renomination in 1916; returned to his ranch near Comanche, Texas, where he engaged in agricultural pursuits and stock raising, and also in the practice of law in Comanche; died in Comanche, Texas, January 31.

•CAMPBELL, THOMAS MITCHELL (1856-1923), twenty-third governor of Texas (1907-11), was born in Rusk, Texas, only the second governor to be a native Texan. His parents were *Thomas Duncan and Rachel Moore Campbell*, who sent him to public schools in town. He also studied at the Rusk Masonic Institute and then at Trinity University at Tehuacana. He began work at the county clerk's office at Longview and studied law at night until he was admitted to the bar in 1878. He was soon regarded as one of the top lawyers in the growing state, and in 1889 he was appointed master in chancery in an International and Great Northern Railroad Company receivership case. In 1891, the rail company hired him as its private counsel, and two years later he was manager of the improved railroad. He resumed his law practice at Palestine in 1897 and became increasingly active in Democratic Party activities. It wasn't until 1907, however, that he ran for public office, he was elected governor by a healthy margin and immediately undertook reform measures in Texas government. His bold and progressive policies woke the opposition of certain wealthy and influential businessmen. However, Campbell saw that immense corporate properties were wholly escaping taxation, so he helped institute a new gross receipts law and an intangible assets law to bring more money into the depleted state budget. Funds were then provided to keep public schools open for at least six months out of the year, and money went to improve all educational facilities in the state. Instead of crippling legitimate enterprises and preventing an influx of capital and population as many had predicted, business became more prosperous than ever before. Campbell also created new state departments to deal with the new issues and problems of the booming state. Departments of insurance and banking, agriculture, labor, taxes and libraries were instituted. He also insured that leasing of prisoners would no longer be allowed in Texas. The governor tried to bring about many other reforms, such as the simplification of the court procedure and cheaper railroad fares, but was prevented by strong business and government opposition. Campbell won easily in 1908 for a second term, and continued working on reforms. He moved back to Palestine, Texas in 1911, and never held elective office again although he tried in 1916 for a U.S. Senate seat. He was on the Exemption Board during World War I. Campbell died in Galveston, and was buried in his home town.

•CASEY, ROBERT (BOB)RANDOLPH, (1915-)- U. S. Representative, Democrat, of Houston, Texas; was born in Joplin, Mo., July 27; son of Sam R. and Mabel E. Casey; moved to Houston, Texas 1930, and graduated from San Jacinto High School; attended the University of Houston and the South Texas School of Law at night; was admitted to the State bar of Texas in 1940; opened law office in Alvin, Texas, and served as city attorney and also a member of the school board; returned to Houston as an assistant district attorney in Harris County, in charge of the civil department; in 1948 was elected to the State house of representatives and served in the regular and special sessions of the 51st Legislature; elected county judge of Harris County in 1950 for a 2-year term; reelected in 1952 and again in 1954 for a 4-year term; member, First Christian Church; married Hazel Marian Brann on August 13, 1935, and have 10 children - Hazel Mary, Robert, Jr., Catherine, Bonnie, Mike, Shawn, Bridget, Eileen, Timothy, and Kevin; elected from the newly created 22d district to the 86th Congress on November 4, 1958; reelected to the 87th, 88th, 89th, 90th, 91st, 92d, and 93rd Congresses.

•CHILTON, HORACE, (1853-1932) (grandson of Thomas Chilton)- U. S. Senator, was born near Tyler, Smith County, Texas, December 29; received private instructions; attended the local schools in Texas and Lynnland Institute, Glendale, Ky.; learned the printing business and at the age of eighteen published a tri-weekly newspaper in Tyler; studied law; was admitted to the bar in 1872 and commenced practice in Tyler, Texas; delegate to the Democratic National Conventions in 1888 and 1896; appointed assistant attorney general of Texas by Governor Roberts in 1881 and served until 1883; appointed to the United States Senate to fill the vacancy caused by the resignation of John H. Reagan and served from June 10, 1891 to March 22, 1892, when a successor was elected; unsuccessful candidate for election to this vacancy; elected as a Democrat to the United States Senate and served from March 4, 1895 to March 3, 1901; was a candidate for reelection in 1900 but in April of that year withdrew; after a long illness he resumed the practice of law in Tyler and Beaumont, Texas; moved to Dallas, Texas, in 1906 and continued the practice of law; died in Dallas, Texas, June 12.

•**CLARK, EDWARD** (1815-80), seventh governor of Texas (1861), was born in Wilkes County, Georgia. His parents were *John*, the Georgia governor in 1819-23, and *Nancy Williamson Clark*. When his father died in 1832, he and his mother moved to Montgomery, Alabama, but soon afterwards he moved to Texas with his first wife. He had attended public schools and knew enough law to be admitted to the bar in Texas. He lived in Marshall and soon became prominent in politics. His first notable public service was at the 1845 constitutional convention for the state, where he was a delegate. He was secretary to the state legislature during its first session, and a senator during its second. He was married again to the former *Martha M. Evans* in 1849, and a few years later was elected secretary of state under *Governor Pease*. Clark was the state commissioner of claims in 1858, before taking the lieutenant governorship the next year. In the bitter controversy over the question of secession early in 1861, *Houston's* strenuous opposition to the movement and his refusal to swear allegiance to the Confederacy caused his removal from office, and Lieutenant Governor Clark was sworn in in March. Texas had officially joined the Confederates, and Governor Clark issued a proclamation on June 8 declaring that a state of war existed. Over 2,000 United States soldiers scattered throughout Texas were forced to surrender, and their arms were confiscated. When Governor Clark's term ended in late 1861, he returned to his home in Marshall, but raised the Fourteenth Texas Infantry for the Confederate States Army. When his side lost the War, Clark escaped to Mexico for a few months but returned to his hometown to resume his practice of law.

•**CLARK, TOM** (1899-), Supreme Court Justice, was born in Dallas, Texas in 1899. He was educated at the Virginia Military Institute and the University of Texas, where he received his law degree. After service in World War I, Mr. Clark practiced law, and was eventually appointed Attorney General by President Truman. Justice Clark was married and had children.

•CLARK, WILLIAM THOMAS, (1831-1905)- U. S. Representative, was born in Norwalk, Conn., June 29; self-educated; taught school in Norwalk, Conn., in 1846; studied law in New York City; was admitted to the bar in 1855 and commenced practice in Davenport, Iowa, the same year; during the Civil War served in the Union Army; commissioned first lieutenant and adjutant of the Thirteenth Iowa Infantry November 2, 1861; captain and assistant adjutant general March 6, 1862; major and adjutant general November 24, 1862; lieutenant colonel and assistant adjutant general, assigned, February 10, 1863, to April 22, 1865; brevetted brigadier general of volunteers July 22, 1864, "for gallant and distinguished services at the Battle of Atlanta, Ga.," and major general November 24, 1865, "for gallant and meritorious services during the war"; mustered out February 1, 1866; engaged in banking in Galveston, Texas; upon the readmission of the State of Texas to representation was elected as a Republican to the Forty-first Congress and served from March 31, 1870, to March 3, 1871; presented credentials as a Member-elect to the Forty-second Congress and served from March 4, 1871, to May 13, 1872, when he was succeeded by De Witt C. Giddings, who contested his election; postmaster of Galveston from June 19, 1872, to May 7, 1874; employed in various offices of the Government at Washington from 1876 to April 12, 1880, when he became chief clerk of the Internal Revenue Department, serving until June 30, 1883; moved to Fargo (now in North Dakota) in 1883 and continued the practice of law; also served as assistant editor of the Fargo Daily Argus; moved to Denver, Colo., in 1890 and practiced law; went to Washington, D. C., in 1898 and was employed in the Internal Revenue Service as a special inspector and served until his death in a hospital in New York City, N. Y., October 12.

•CLEMENTS, WILLIAM P. (1917-), forty-first governor of Texas (1979-83), was born in Dallas, Texas and attended the Highland Park High School near that city. He studied at Southern Methodist University, and after his 1937 graduation began working as a roughneck and driller in the oil fields of northeast Texas. He gained experience on the rigs and within 10 years had the capital to found SEDCO, an offshore drilling platform company that eventually became very successful. Clements also married the former *Rita Crocker* during this time, and began a family of two children. In a Democratic-dominated state, Clements became active in the Republican Party. He was a conservative with a growing income from SEDCO and other involvements with various Texas banks and the Keebler Company. He was also active in the Boy Scouts of America, eventually becoming president of the Circle Ten Council, and later a member of the National Executive Board of that organization. In 1965 to 1973, Clements was chair of the Board of Governors of Southern Methodist University. He continues to hold a seat on that board today. His involvement with the Republican Party earned him a good reputation. In 1973, *President Ford* named him a deputy secretary of Defense, one of the highest-level jobs in Washington. He served four years, receiving a Department of Defense Medal for Distinguished Public Service in 1975, and a Bronze Palm award from the President in 1976. These successes made Clements a well-known figure in Texas, and after his term in Washington, he began to consider running for governor. With a large amount of confidence and money ($7 million dollars went into his campaign), he won over Democratic favorite *John Hill* in 1978, the first Republican to do so since the Reconstruction. This did much to encourage the growth of the Republicans in the state, which was especially evident in 1980, when a fellow southerner *Jimmy Carter* was defeated by the Texans in favor of Republican *Ronald Reagan*. Although Clements has not accomplished all of the tax-cutting measures he promised, he held the favor of a majority of the Texas voters until the election of 1982.

•COCKRELL, JEREMIAH VARDAMAN, (1832-1915) (brother of Francis Marion Cockrell)- U. S. Representative, was born near Warrensburg, Johnson County, Mo., May 7; attended the common schools and Chapel Hill College, Lafayette County, Mo.; went to California in 1849; returned to Missouri in 1853; engaged in agricultural pursuits and studied law; entered the Confederate Army as a lieutenant and served throughout the Civil War, attaining the rank of colonel; at the close of the war he settled in Sherman, Grayson County, Texas, and engaged in the practice of law; chief justice of Grayson County in 1872; delegate to the Democratic State conventions in 1878 and 1889; moved to Jones County; appointed judge of the thirty-ninth judicial district court in 1885, to which position he was elected in 1886 and reelected in 1890; elected as a Democrat to the Fifty-third and Fifty-fourth Congresses (Mar. 4, 1893-Mar. 3, 1897); was not a candidate for renomination in 1896; engaged in farming and stock raising in Jones County, Texas; died in Abilene, Texas on March 18.

•COKE, RICHARD (1829-1897), fourteenth governor of Texas (1874-76), was born in Williamsburg, Virginia, the son of *John and Eliza Coke*. He attended public schools and at 16 he entered William and Mary College from which he graduated in 1849. The next year he completed his law studies and moved to Waco, Texas to begin a practice. He married *Marie Horne* in 1852 and settled into a quiet life until the outbreak of the Civil War; he was a secessionist and joined the Confederate Army. At the close of the war, he retired as a captain and returned to his law practice. He was appointed a district judge in 1865 and the next year was elected a justice of the Texas Supreme Court. *General Philip Sheridan* removed him from this last post, however, because he was thought to be an "impediment to Reconstruction". The Democrats in Texas only respected him more after this, and soon he was regarded as a leader in the white conservative backlash against *Sheridan's* policies. As the Democrats began to regain power in the legislature, Coke was able to win the governorship in late 1873. He was inaugurated late one night in mid-January, but had difficulty beginning his administration since the former governor refused to leave office. Coke nevertheless began to replace radical Republicans with his conservative friends in state government posts. The first constitution imposed by Reconstructionist military authority was replaced under Coke's rule in 1875. Coke also was able to control outlaw and Indian raids on the frontier by assigning the Texas Rangers to roam the state and fight for justice, although their methods were not always fair. Governor Coke finished his term in Austin and was elected to the U.S. Senate, where he served for 18 years. He returned to Waco and lived there in retirement to his death.

•COLEMAN, RONALD D, (1941-)- U. S. Representative, Democrat, of El Paso, Texas, was born in El Paso on November 29; attended public schools of El Paso; graduated, Austin High School, El Paso, 1959; B.A., University of Texas at El Paso, 1963; J.D., University of Texas School of Law, 1967; attended University of Kent, Canterbury, England, 1981; admitted to the Texas Bar, 1969; attorney; teacher, El Paso public schools, 1967; served in U.S. Army, captain, 1967-69, Army Commendation Medal; assistant county attorney, 1969; first assistant county attorney, 1971; elected to Texas Legislature, 1973-82; member: American and El Paso Associations; delegate: Texas Constitutional Convention, 1974, State Democratic Convention, four times; honors and awards: State Bar of Texas Administration of Justice Award, 1973, Environmental Award - Sierra Club, 1977, Texas Association of School Administrators and School Boards Award for Education, 1977, Texas Compensatory Education Association Certificate of Recognition, 1979, State Bar of Texas State Bar Legislative Award, 1979; married to the former Tammy Beil; one child, Kimberly Michelle; elected on November 2, 1982 to the 98th Congress.

•COLLINS, JAMES M., (1916-)- U. S. Representative, Republican, of Irving, Texas; was born in Hallsville, April 29; attended Woodrow Wilson High School, Dallas; graduated from Southern Methodist University, B.S.C., and chosen Representative Mustang, 1937; Northwestern University, winner of Outstanding Achievement Award, M.B.A., cum laude, 1938; American College, C.L.U., 1940; Harvard Business School, president of student body, M.B.A., 1943; 3 1/2 years in the U.S. Army; completed service as captain, U.S. Army Engineers; 1 1/2 years in the European theater from Omaha Beach through France, Belgium, and Germany; received four battle stars and Medal of Metz; president, Consolidated Industries, Inc., and International Industries, Inc., home office Dallas, Texas; president Fidelity Union Life Insurance Co., 1954-65; active in civic affairs, including Greater Dallas Planning Council, Salvation Army, Military Order of World War; president, Dallas Council on World Affairs; distinguished SMU alumnus 1971; 1971 Man of Year by

Federation of Independent Business; White House Conference on Youth; American Legion, VFW, Chamber of Commerce, Heart Association, TB Association, United Fund, Dallas Assembly, Big Brothers, YPO, Park Cities Baptist Church, Phi Delta Theta, national president SMU Alumni Association, Trustee on Board SMU; married Dorothy Dann of Maplewood, N.J., September 16, 1942; three children: Michael James, Dorothy Colville (Mrs. David Weaver), and Nancy Miles (Mrs. Richard Fisher); elected to the 90th Congress August 24, 1968, in special election; reelected to 91st, 92d, and 93rd Congresses.

•COLQUITT, OSCAR B. (1861-1940), twenty-fourth governor of Texas (1911-15), was born in Camilla, Georgia, the son of *Thomas J. and Ann Burkhalter Colquitt.* He lived on the family plantation until his father went bankrupt in 1878 and moved to Texas to work as a tenant farmer. Young Oscar then worked as a railroad station porter and later turned it into a furniture factory. He attended public school in Daingerfield, Texas, and then the private academy in town. Deciding to learn a printer's trade, Colquitt obtained a job at the Morris County *Banner* newspaper. In 1884, he founded his own paper, the Pittsburg (Texas) *Gazette.* Two years later he sold this paper to a younger brother and purchased the Terrell (Texas) *Star.* During these years in journalism, he also had a share in establishing the first cotton seed mill in Texas, erected at Pittsburgh in 1885. In 1888 he founded the First National Bank of Terrell. His interest in politics was stimulated by editorial work, and in 1890 he was made chair of the Kaufman County Democratic organization. He was elected to the state senate in 1895, and as a state revenue agent for eight months in 1898. In 1899-1900, after his senate term was up, he was on the state tax commission. He had sold his newspaper in 1897 and became active in oil development in the Corsicana area. In 1902 he was elected to the state railroad commission; reelected in 1908. His reorganization of the state transportation system led to his election as governor. Colquitt continued the reforms Campbell initiated of the state prison system. He refused to submit the question of prohibition to the legislature and brought on the wrath of the Methodist church. He was also opposed when he supported Germany in the early stages of World War I. However, he was reelected in 1912. In his second term, he approved a parole system and created a Bureau of Child and Animal Protection. He was forced to call out the Texas National Guard in several occasions to patrol the Mexican border as the Revolution erupted there. Colquitt left Austin to try to win a U.S. Senate seat, but was unsuccessful. He resumed his oil business and worked his farm near Dallas. In 1928, he headed the anti-Smith faction of the Democratic Party in Texas, and was *President Hoover's* appointee to the U.S. Board of Mediation where he served until 1933. After that, he was a member of the railway division of the Reconstruction Finance Corporation, holding that post until he died in Dallas.

•COMBS, JESSE MARTIN, (1889-1953)- U. S. Representative, was born in Center, Shelby County, Texas, July 7; attended the public schools; was graduated from Southwest Texas State Teachers' College in 1912; was admitted to the bar in 1918 and commenced practice in Kountze, Texas; county judge of Hardin County, Texas, in 1919 and 1920; district judge of the seventy-fifth district 1923-1925; associate justice of the ninth court of civil appeals 1933-1943; member and president of the board of trustees of South Park Schools 1926-1940; president of the board of trustees of Lamar College 1940-1944; elected as a Democrat to the Seventy-ninth and to the three succeeding Congresses (January 3, 1945-January 3, 1953); was not a candidate for renomination in 1952; returned to Beaumont, Texas, where he died August 21.

•CONNALLY, JOHN BOWDEN (1917-), thirty-eighth governor of Texas (1963-69), was born in Floresville, Texas, the son of *John Bowden and Lila Wright Connally.* His family was poor, but young John helped build the ranch into an 8,000 acre cattle operation that has since made him a multi-millionaire. He graduated from the University of Texas in 1941, soon after he had married *Idanell Brill.* He received a law degree and practiced in his home town until he became president and general manager of KVET Radio in Austin. Senator *Lyndon B. Johnson* hired him as an assistant in 1949, and at the same time he joined a law partnership in Austin. Oilmen *Sid Richardson* and *Perry Bass* hired him as their personal attorney in 1952, where he learned a great deal about making money. He left their Fort Worth operation in 1961 to become *President Kennedy's* Secretary of the Navy. That position only lasted 11 months, however, since he was elected governor of Texas in 1962. Connally, although a Democrat, vowed to cut back on funding for the aged, poor, and education. He also promised to cut the state budget by 10 percent but by the end of his terms, the state budget had increased by 63 percent. He also hired more women and minorities than any previous governors, and reformed the state penal code. In 1963, Connally was wounded at the scene of *John F. Kennedy's* assassination, which heightened the voters sympathy in the next election. The governor continued to increase support for welfare programs in the state, despite his vocal opposition to it. He also created a Texas Tourist Bureau, which helped begin a large immigration to the state. Connally was elected to two more terms, but declined a fourth. He then joined a law firm in Houston, where he worked for two years until his appointment as *President Nixon's* Secretary of Defense. In 1973, he was made a special advisor to the President, the same year he switched parties to become a Republican. Before Nixon resigned, Connally returned to Houston to work at his former law firm. In July 1974 he was indicted by a Watergate jury for taking $10,000 from the Associated Milk Producers, Inc., the largest U.S. dairy cooperative, and for covering up the crime. He was acquitted of all charges in 1975, however, and returned to his Houston law office. In 1979, Connally announced his candidacy for U.S. President, but lost in the Republican primary to Ronald Reagan. He continues to reside in Houston, but visits his Floresville ranch from time to time. He and his wife have three children.

•CONNALLY, THOMAS TERRY (TOM), (1877-1963)- U. S. Representative and U. S. Senator, was born near Hewitt, McLennan County, Texas, August 19; attended the public schools and Eddy (Tex.) High School; was graduated from Baylor University, Waco, Texas, in 1896 and from the law department of the University of Texas at Austin in 1898; was admitted to the bar in 1898 and commenced practice in Waco, Texas; moved to Marlin,

Falls County, Texas, in 1899 and continued the practice of law; served as sergeant major in the Second Regiment, Texas Volunteer Infantry, during the Spanish american War; member of the State house of representatives 1901-1904; prosecuting attorney of Falls County, Texas, 1906-1910; during the First World War became captain and adjutant of the Twenty-second Infantry Brigade, Eleventh Division, United States Army, in 1918; delegate to the Democratic National Conventions in 1920, 1932, 1936, 1940, and 1948, serving as chairman of Texas delegation in 1936 and as vice chairman in 1948; permanent chairman of Texas Democratic State convention in 1938; delegate to the Inter-parliamentary Union at Geneva in 1924, at London in 1930, at Constantinople in 1934, and at Rome 1948; delegate to Empire Parliamentary Association at Ottawa in 1943; special congressional adviser to the United States delegation to the Inter-American conference on Problems of War and Peace at Mexico City in 1945; member and vice chairman of the United States delegation to the United Nations Conference on International Organization at San Francisco in 1945; representative of the United States to the first session of the General Assembly of the United Nations at London and to the second session at New York in 1946; adviser to the Secretary of State at the meetings of the Council of Foreign Ministers at Paris and New York and at the Paris Peace Conference in 1946; delegate to the Inter-American conference for the maintenance of Continental Peace and Security at Rio de Janeiro in 1947; elected as a Democrat to the Sixty-fifth and to the five succeeding Congresses (March 4, 1917-March 3, 1929); did not seek renomination in 1928, having become a candidate for Senator; elected to the United States Senate in 1928; reelected in 1934, 1940, and again in 1946 and served from March 4, 1929, to January 3, 1953, was not a candidate for renomination in 1952; engaged in the practice of law in Washington, D. C., where he died October 28.

•CONNER, JOHN COGGSWELL, (1842-1873)- U. S. Representative, was born in Noblesville, Hamilton County, Ind., October 14; attended the Noblesville public schools and Wabash College, Crawfordsville, Ind.; admitted to the United States Naval Academy, Annapolis, Md., September 20, 1861, and remained during the academic year, 1861-1862; during the Civil War was commissioned a second lieutenant in the Sixty-third Regiment, Indiana Volunteer Infantry, on August 30, 1862, and a first lieutenant on September 3, 1862; honorably discharged June 20, 1864k; unsuccessful candidate for election to the Indiana House of Representatives in 1866; commissioned a captain in the Forty-first Regiment, United States Infantry, on July 28, 1866, and served in Texas until November 29, 1869, when he resigned, having received the nomination for Congress; upon the readmission of Texas to representation was elected as a Democrat to the Forty-first Congress; reelected to the Forty-second Congress and served from March 31, 1870, to March 3, 1873; owing to failing health was not a candidate for renomination in 1872; died in Washington D. C., December 10, 1873; interment in the Old Cemetery, Noblesville, Ind.

•COOPER, SAMUEL BRONSON, (1850-1918)- U. S. Representative, born near Eddyville, Caldwell County, Ky., May 30; moved with his parents to Texas the same year and located in Woodville, Tyler County; attended the common schools; studied law; was admitted to the bar in 1871 and commenced practice in Woodville in January 1872; prosecuting attorney of Tyler County 1876-1880; member of the State senate 1880-1884; appointed collector of internal revenue for the first district of Texas by President Cleveland in 1885 and served until 1888; unsuccessful candidate for district judge in 1888; elected as a Democrat to the Fifty-third and to the five succeeding Congresses (March 4, 1893-March 3, 1905); unsuccessful candidate for reelection to the Fifty-ninth Congress; again elected to the Sixtieth Congress (March 4, 1907-March 3, 1909); unsuccessful candidate for reelection to the Sixty-first Congress; appointed a member of the United States Board of General Appraisers at the port of New York City by President Taft in 1910; died in New York City August 21; interment in Magnolia Cemetery, Beaumont, Jefferson County, Texas.

•CORDON, GUY, (1890-1969)- U. S. Senator, was born in Cuero, De Witt County, Texas, April 24; moved to Roseburg, Oregon and attended the public schools of Oregon; deputy assessor, 1909-1916; county assessor of Douglas County, Oregon, 1917-1920; during the First World War served as a private in the Field Artillery of the United States Army in 1918; was admitted to the bar in 1920 and commenced practice in Roseburg, Oregon; district attorney of Douglas County 1923-1935; appointed and subsequently elected as a Republican to the United States Senate to fill the vacancy caused by the death of Charles L. McNary; reelected in 1948 and served from March 4, 1944 to January 3, 1955; unsuccessful candidate for reelection in 1954; engaged in the practice of law in Washington, D. C., until his retirement in 1962; died in Washington, D. C., June 8.

•CRAIN, WILLIAM HENRY, (1848-1896)- U. S. Representative, was born in Galveston, Texas, November 25; attended the Christian Brothers' School, New York City, until the age of fourteen, and was graduated from St. Francis Xavier's College, New York City, in 1867; returned to Texas and lived on a ranch for two years; studied law in Indianola, Texas, while teaching school; was admitted to the bar in 1871 and commenced practice in Indianola, Texas; member of the State senate 1876-1878; district attorney of the twenty-third judicial district of Texas 1872-1876; elected as a Democrat to the Forty-ninth and to the five succeeding Congresses and served from March 4, 1885, until his death in Washington, D. C., February 10.

•CRANE, ROYSTON CAMPBELL (1901-), cartoonist, was born November 22, 1901 in Abilene, Texas. He was educated at Hardin-Simmons university, Chicago Academy of Fine Arts, and the University of Texas. Upon graduation he worked in the art department of several newspapers including the New York World. He started the popular comic strip *Wash Tubbs* and *Capitan Easy* which ran from 1924 until 1943. In that year he began the famous *Buz Sawyer* strip which was syndicated nationally. Mr Crane has received many awards for his work including the Reuban award of the National Cartoonist Society, Gold Medal for Public Service from U.S. Navy, and silver lady award from Banshees as outstanding cartoonist of the year. He is married and has two children.

•CRANFORD, JOHN WALTER, (1862-1899)- U. S. Representative, was born near Grove Hill, Clarke County, Ala.; attended the common and high schools of Alabama and finished preparatory studies under a private tutor; moved to Texas about 1880 and settled at Sulphur Springs; studied law; was admitted to the bar and commenced practice in Texas; member of the State senate 1888-1896; elected president pro tempore of the twenty-second senate; elected as a Democrat to the Fifty-fifth Congress and served from March 4, 1897, until his death in Washington, D. C., March 3.

•CROCKETT, DAVID (1786-1836), was born in Limestone, Tennessee, and became familiar with the outdoors at an early age. When he was only 13, he left home to trap furs in West Tennessee and Virginia, but returned in 1801 to help his father pay off debts. He married in 1809 and lived in Tennessee for the next several years, serving in the Creek Indian War of 1813-14. He was a respected member of his Franklin County, Tennessee community, and was elected to the state legislature in 1821 and 1823. After moving to Gibson County, Crockett became known as a fearless bear fighter, having killed over 100 of the animals. He was elected to the U.S. Congress in 1828, where he served until 1831. Representative Crockett opposed *President Jackson's* policies toward the Indians and supported squatters' rights in West Tennessee. In 1832 he was once more a member of the state legislature, he was very popular with his fellow-Tennesseeans; his down-home language and humor as well as his determination made him a legend in many areas besides the south. Crockett once advised his admirers to "Be sure you are right, then go ahead." He applied this guideline when he decided to help the Anglo-Texans gain independence from Mexico. In the manner of his characterization of himself as "half a horse and half an alligator with a touch of a snapping turtle," Crockett helped defend the Alamo at San Antonio, Texas against the Mexican army. He was killed along with the 180 other men on March 6, 1836. His autobiography, *A Narrative of the Life of Davy Crockett*, was published in 1834.

•CROSS, OLIVER HARLAN, (1868-1960)- U. S. Representative, was born in Eutaw, Greene County, Ala., July 13; attended the public schools and was graduated from the University of Alabama at Tuscaloosa in 1891; teacher in the public schools at Union Springs, Ala., in 1891 and 1892; studied law; was admitted to the bar in 1893 and commenced practice in Deming, N. Mex.; moved to McGregor, Texas, in 1894 and continued the practice of law; served as city attorney of McGregor in 1895 and 1896; moved to Waco, Texas, in 1896 and continued the practice of law; assistant attorney of McLennan County 1898-1902; member of the State house of representatives in 1900; district attorney of McLennan County 1902-1906; retired from law practice in 1917 and assumed agricultural pursuits; elected as a Democrat to the Seventy-first and to the three succeeding Congresses (March 4, 1929-January 3, 1937); was not a candidate for renomination in 1936; engaged in agricultural pursuits and in real-estate activities; died in Waco, Texas, April 24.

•CROWLEY, MILES, (1859-1921)- U. S. Representative, was born in Boston, Mass., February 22; attended the common schools; employed as a longshoreman; moved to Galveston in the seventies; assistant chief of the Galveston Fire Department; studied law; was admitted to the bar in 1892 and commenced practice; member of the State house of representatives in 1892; served in the State senate in 1893 and 1894; elected as a Democrat to the Fifty-fourth Congress (March 4, 1895-March 3, 1897); was not a candidate for reelection in 1896; resumed the practice of law in Galveston, Texas; prosecuting attorney of Galveston County 1904-1912; elected judge of Galveston County Court in 1920, in which capacity he was serving at the time of his death in Galveston, Texas, on September 22.

•CULBERSON, CHARLES A. (1855-1925), twentieth governor of Texas (1895-99), was born in Dadeville, Alabama, to *David B. and Eugenia Kimball Culberson*. The parents moved to Gilmer, Texas when Charles was only three, and eventually his father represented his district in Congress. He attended public schools in his neighborhood and entered the Virginia Military Institute in Lexington, Virginia in 1870. After graduating in 1874 he began to study law with his father and then at the University of Virginia. By 1882 he was an active lawyer, and had married the former *Sallie Harrison*. He set up an office in Jefferson, Texas, but moved to Dallas in 1887. In the meantime, he was justice of the peace for Wood County, and was attorney for the county in 1876. He was also District Attorney in 1880 and 1882. At the Democratic State Convention in 1890 he was nominated for attorney general of Texas, a position he won by a large majority. He served in that seat until his election as governor four years later. Governor Culberson recommended an increase in the school tax in the state, and called a special legislative session to prohibit the prize fight between *Robert Fitzsimmons* and *James Corbett* in Texas. The Spanish-American War began during Culberson's second term, and he was concerned with building up the state's defenses. Culberson was elected to the U.S. Senate, and served there in 1899 to 1923. He was an active Democrat throughout his career. Although he died in Washington D.C., he was buried at Fort Worth, Texas.

•CULBERSON, DAVID BROWNING, (1830-1900) (father of Charles Allen Culberson)- U. S. Representative, was born in Troup County, Ga., September 29; pursued preparatory studies in Brownwood College, LaGrange, Ga.; studied law; was admitted to the bar in 1851 and commenced practice in Dadeville, Ala.; moved to Texas in 1856; settled in Jefferson, Marion County, in 1861 and continued the practice of law; member of the State house of representatives in 1859; during the Civil War entered the Confederate Army as a private; promoted to the rank of colonel of the Eighteenth Texas Infantry; assigned to duty in 1864 as adjutant general of the State of Texas with the rank of colonel; again a member of the State house of representatives in 1864; elected to the State senate in 1873 and served until his resignation, having been elected to Congress; elected as a Democrat to the Forty-fourth and to the town succeeding Congresses (March 4, 1875-March 3, 1897); declined to be a candidate for renomination in 1896; appointed by President McKinley on June 21, 1897, as one of the commissioners to codify the laws of the United States and served in this capacity until his death in Jefferson, Texas, May 7.

D

•**DANIEL, MARION PRICE** (1910-), thirty-seventh governor of Texas (1957-63), was born in Dayton, Texas, the son of *Marion Price and Nannie Partlow Daniels*. He studied at public schools at Liberty and Fort Worth, Texas before entering Baylor University. He received his A.B. in 1931 and his L.L.B. from that institution in 1932. Before college, he had worked at the Fort Worth *Star-Telegram* as a reporter for a year, and for the Waco *News Tribune* for two years while he was a student. Once admitted to the bar in 1932, he left journalism to work as a lawyer in Liberty. In 1938, he was elected to the state legislature, becoming speaker of the house in 1943. Soon afterwards, however, he joined the Army to serve in the second World War. He enlisted as a private, but was made a captain before his discharge in 1946. In November of that year, he was elected attorney general of Texas, and soon after moved to Austin. In that position, he succeeded in prosecuting gambling wire service operators and major drug dealers. He also defended the state during the Texas tidelands controversy with the federal government. He published such essays as "Texas Ownership of Submerged Lands," and "Ownership of the Continental Shelf," which made him an expert on legal rights to tidelands. In 1953, he took his elected seat on the U.S. Senate, where he served until taking office as governor in 1957. He was a member of the interstate and foreign commerce committee as well as the judiciary committee in the senate and continued his fight for Texas rights to lease offshore lands. As governor, Daniel supported water conservation and irrigation projects; more than 40 dams and reservoirs were built during his six year term. He also signed bills appropriating more money to both elementary and higher education. He created a Texas Youth Council and a Texas Law Enforcement Commission. The governor also encouraged more controls on lobbyists and insurance companies in the state. During the third term, Daniel approved a

53

state sales tax to offset the costs of all of his new projects. He lost in his attempt for a fourth term in 1962, and returned to his law practice, this time in Austin. Since 1971, he has been a justice on the Texas Supreme Court, and makes his home in Liberty, Texas.

•DAVIS, EDMUND J. (1827-1882), thirteenth governor of Texas (1870-74), was born in Florida near St. Augustine. When his father died, he moved with his mother to Galveston, Texas in 1848. He studied law and entered into a practice there and in Laredo, Corpus Christi and Brownsville. As deputy collector of customs on the Rio Grande in 1850-52, he got his first taste of public affairs, and soon after he was appointed a district attorney and judge of the district court of Austin (1853 and 1855). Davis was opposed to secession, so he retired his office and left the state. He joined the Union forces and organized a regiment of cavalry to fight in Louisiana and south Texas, attaining the rank of brigadier general by the close of the war. At one point, when he was recruiting men at Matamoras, Mexico, he was captured and nearly executed by Confederate soldiers, but was able to escape. Davis joined the Republican Party after the war and immediately became involved in Reconstruction efforts. He was a member of the first Reconstruction Convention of 1866 and was one of the "Radicals" who insisted on the "iron-clad oath" for former Confederates who wished to vote. The few voters left over elected him governor in 1869. Governor Davis had the support of the state legislature, which had 11 black members out of 120. However, his opponents were outraged at Davis' vengeful actions and began making charges of corruption. Five of the governor's measures, referred to as "obnoxious acts" by the Democrats were passed; he authorized an act permitting the governor to proclaim martial law and to suspend *habeas corpus* ; also laws organizing a state police force and requiring the "iron clad oath" for voters, and allowing the governor to appoint more than 8,000 persons to formerly elected positions in the state government. The people of Texas resented the imposition of martial law and the greater freedom given to the state police. In Davis' first 14 months of office, 3,475 people had been arrested, and the use of black policemen outraged the conservative whites. That Governor

Davis also supported progress in railroading and allowed for every married settler to receive a grant of 160 acres from the government for homesteading did not bring back the public favor, and he was outvoted by Democrats in the next election. The new legislature had overturned Governor Davis' strict voting requirements, so the election of *Richard Coke* was made possible. However, Davis refused to leave office, claiming that the vote was illegal, and called upon the federal government for assistance. For three months, there were two governments in Austin. Only when it was clear that *President Grant* would not support Davis against *Coke* did the defeated governor leave office. He moved into his private home in Austin and practiced law there until his death. He was buried at the state cemetery with full military and civic honors.

•DAVIS, JAMES HARVEY (CYCLONE), (1853-1940)- U. S. Representative, was born near Walhalla, Pickens District, S. C., December 24; moved to Texas with his parents, who settled in Wood County, near Winnsboro, in 1857; attended the common schools; taught school from 1875 to 1878; elected judge of Franklin County in 1878; studied law; was admitted to the bar in 1882 and commenced practice in Mount Vernon, Texas; lecturer for the Farmers' Alliance for three years; engaged in the newspaper publishin business; president of the Texas Press Association 1886-1888; unsuccessful Populist candidate for attorney general of Texas in 1892; was influential in the formation of the Populist Party and served as organizer and committeeman from 1892 to 1900; unsuccessful populist candidate for election in 1894 to the Fifty-fourth Congress; declined the appointment as superintendent of agriculture for the Philippine Islands in 1914; elected as a Democrat to the Sixty-fourth Congress (March 4, 1915-March 3, 1917); unsuccessful candidate for renomination in 1916 to the Sixty-Fifth Congress; returned to his home in Sulphur Springs, Hopkins County, Texas, and engaged in agricultural pursuits and Chautauqua work; moved to Kaufman, Texas, in 1935, where he died on January 31.

•DEBAKEY, MICHAEL E. (1908 -), surgeon and heart-transplant pioneer, was born in Lake Charles, Louisiana, son of Lebanese immigrants who spoke French. Early on, he took an interest in biology, and after graduation from high school, he studied science at Tulane University in New Orleans. He obtained a B.S. degree in 1930, and then went on to study for an M.D., which he received two years later. At Tulane, he was influenced by blood vessel surgeons, and did his internship at Tulane surgical service in 1933-35. Afterwards, he studied at the University at Strasbourg, France and Heidelberg, Germany. He returned to Tulane as an instructor in 1937, and by 1946 had been named associate professor of surgery. Houston's Baylor University hired him as a full professor of surgery as well as chairman of the department at its medical school in 1948. He had served on the surgical consultants division during World War II, and had investigated arterial and chest wounds. This inspired him to develop a means to transplant other blood vessels in place of damaged ones, which also helped victims of aneurisms and "hardening of the arteries." In 1956, DeBakey developed plastic tubing that could be used in place of real blood vessels in such surgery. Before long, DeBakey and his associates were investigating ways to transplant a heart. He devised his own surgical instruments for this research. In 1959, his findings carried him to the Soviet Union where he conferred with other surgeons and worked to establish a U.S. -Soviet research project for heart disease. An early warner about the dangers of smoking, DeBakey has been concerned about the level of health in society. He has served on the National Research Council, and on advisory groups to the U.S. Surgeon General and National Institute of Health. In 1966, DeBakey became world-famous when he implanted the first artificial heart in a man at Baylor. He has continued his research and operations at Baylor University at Houston, Texas in recent years.

•DEGENER, EDWARD, (1809-1890)- U. S. Representative, was born in Brunswick, Germany, October 20; pursued an academic course in Germany and in England; twice a member of the legislative body in Anhalt-Dessau and a member of the first German National Assembly in Frankfort on the Main in 1848; immigrated to the United States in 1850 and located in Sisterdale, Kendall County, Texas; engaged in agricultural pursuits; during the Civil War was court-martialed and imprisoned by the Confederates because of his devotion to the Union cause; after his release from imprisonment engaged in the wholesale grocery business in San Antonio; member of the Texas constitutional conventions in 1866 and 1868; upon the readmission of the State of Texas to representation was elected as a Republican to the Forty-first Congress and served from March 31, 1870, to March 3, 1871; unsuccessful for reelection in 1870 to the Forty-second Congress; member of the city council of San Antonio, Texas, 1872-1878; died in San Antonio, Texas, September 11; interment in the City Cemetery.

•DE GRAFFENREID, REESE CALHOUN, (1859-1902)- U. S. Representative, was born in Franklin, Williamson County, Tenn., May 7; attended the common schools of Franklin and the University of Tennessee at Knoxville; was graduated from the law department of Cumberland University, Lebanon, Tenn.; was admitted to the bar in 1879 and commenced practice in Franklin; moved to Chattanooga, Tenn., where he practiced his profession for one year, moving thence to Texas; helped in the construction of the Texas & Pacific Railroad; resumed the practice of law at Longview, Texas, in 1883; elected county attorney and resigned two months afterward presidential elector on the Democratic ticket of Cleveland and Thurman in 1888; unsuccessful candidate for election in 1890 to the Fifty-fifth, Fifty-sixth, and Fifty-seventh Congresses and served from March 4, 1897, until his death in Washington, D. C., August 29.

•DE LA GARZA, E (KIKA), (1927-)- U. S. Representative, Democrat, of Mission, Texas; was born in Mercedes, September 22; educated at Mission High School, Edinburg (Texas) Jr. College, and St. Mary's University, San Antonio, Texas; LL.B., J.D., 1952, St. Mary's Law School; during World War II enlisted in the

U.S. Navy, age 17; served in the U.S. Army, 37th Division Artillery, as an officer 1950 to 1952; attorney; married the former Lucille Alamia of Edinburg, Texas; three children: Jorge, Michael, and Angela; Catholic; served in the State house of representatives for 12 years; member of Mission, McAllen, and Rio Grande Valley chamber of commerce; American Legion, Catholic War Veterans (past national judge advocate), Kiwanis, International Good Neighbor Council, Delta Theta Phi, the League of United Latin American Citizens, and honorary member of Pi Sigma Alpha, national political science honor society; elected to the 89th Congress November 3, 1964; reelected to 90th, 91st, 92d, and 93d Congresses.

•**DOBIE, JAMES F.** (1888-1964), author, was born in Live Oak County, Texas, on a ranch. He grew to love the old Spanish lore of South Texas, and was greatly influenced by it in his later writings. He received his B.A. from Southwestern University of Texas in 1910, taught school for a while, and then studied at Columbia University in New York, from which he received an M.A. in English in 1914. He began teaching at the University of Texas, but the outbreak of World War I sent him to France. Returning home safely in 1919, he resumed his teaching career, but soon took some time off to return to ranching. He was chairman of the English department at Oklahoma Agricultural and Mechanical College in 1923-25, and then returned to the University of Texas as an adjunct professor of English. He remained there until his retirement in 1947, eventually receiving full professorship and tenure. The heart of his work was his writing about the Spanish heritage of Texas. His first book, *Vaquero of the Brush Country*, was published in 1929. He continued to collect the local legends of South Texas in *Coronado's Children* (1930), *Tales of the Mustang* (1936), and *Up the Trail from Texas* (1955), among over 25 other books. He was a visiting professor of American history at Cambridge University, England in 1943-44, where he was warmly received. An honorary M.A. degree followed. He wrote about the year in his *A Texan in England* (1945). He was active in the Texas Folklore Society for many years, and was also a contributing editor to the *Southwest Review*. *President Lyndon B. Johnson* awarded him a Medal of Freedom in 1964, shortly before he died at Austin.

•DIES, MARTIN, (1870-1922)- U. S. Representative, was born in Jackson Parish, La., March 13; moved with his parents to Freestone County, Texas, in 1876; attended the common schools and was graduated from the law department of the University of Texas at Austin; was admitted to the bar in 1893 and commenced practice in Woodville, Texas; edited a newspaper in Freestone County; was county marshal; county judge of Tyler County in 1894; district attorney of the first judicial district of Texas 1898-1900; moved to colorado, Texas, and engaged in the practice of law; moved to Beaumont, Texas, in 1902 and was employed as counsel for the Gulf Refining Co.; elected as a Democrat to the Sixty-first and to the four succeeding Congresses (March 4, 1909-March 3, 1919); was not a candidate for reelection in 1918; retired to his ranch on Turkey Creek, Tyler County, Texas; moved to Kerrville, Texas in 1921 and died there July 13.

•DOWDY, JOHN VERNARD, (1912-)- U. S. Representative, was born in Waco, McLennan County, Texas, February 11; spent early years of his youth inRusk, Texas; graduated from high school in Henderson, Texas, in 1928; attended the College of Marshall (now East Texas Baptist College) 1929-1931, then undertook the private study of law and worked as a court reporter 1931-1944; admitted to the bar in 1940 and began practice in Athens, Texas; district attorney, third judicial district of Texas, 1945-1952; elected as a Democrat to the Eighty-second Congress to fill the vacancy caused by the resignation of Tom Pickett; reelected to the Eighty-third and to the eight succeeding Congresses and served from September 23, 1952, to January 3, 1971. Reelected to the Ninety-second Congress.

E

•EAGLE, JOE HENRY, (1870-1963)- U. S. Representative, was born in Tompkinsville, Monroe County, Ky., January 23; was graduated from the local high school in 1883 and obtained a first-grade teacher's certificate in 1884; was also graduated from Burritt College, Spencer, Tenn., in 1887; moved to Texas; taught school 1887-1893 and served as superintendent of the city schools of Vernon, Texas, 1889-1891; studied law at night and during vacations; was admitted to the bar in 1893 and commenced practice in Wichita Falls, Texas; city attorney of Wichita Falls in 1894 and 1895; moved to Houston in 1895 and continued the practice of law; elected as a Democrat to the Sixty-third and to the three succeeding Congresses (March 4, 1913-March 3, 1921); was not a candidate for renomination in 1920; elected on January 28, 1933, to both the Seventy-second and Seventy-third Congresses to fill the vacancies caused by the death of Daniel E. Garrett, who had been reelected in 1932; reelected to the Seventy-fourth Congress and served from January 28, 1933, to January 3, 1937; was not a candidate for renomination in 1936, but was an unsuccessful candidate for the Democratic nomination for United States Senator; resumed the practice of his profession; was a resident of Houston, Texas, until his death January 10.

•ECKHARDT, BOB, (1913-)- U. S. Representative, Democrat, of Harris County, Texas; was born July 16 in Austin; graduated from University of Texas, B.A., 1935; LL.B., 1939; served in the U.S. Army Air Corps; taught at Coleman Flying School, Enlisted Reserve 1942-44; honorable discharge, 1944; practicing attorney until he entered Congress in 1967; served in the Texas House of Representatives 1958-66; married Orissa Stevenson, deceased; children: Orissa and Rosalind; married Nadine Ellen Cannon; children: Sidney, Shelby, William, and Sarah; elected to the 90th

Congress; reelected to 91st, 92d, and 93d Congresses; serves on the Committee on Interstate and Foreign Commerce, and on its Subcommittee on Commerce and Finance; and on the Committee on Merchant Marine and Fisheries, and on its Subcommittees on Fisheries and Wildlife Conservation and the Environment; Merchant Marine; and Oceanography.

•**EISENHOWER, DWIGHT D.** (1890-1969), thirty-fourth President of the U.S., was born in Denison, Texas to *David J. and Ida Stover Eisenhower.* a year later, they moved to Abilene, Kansas, where young Dwight attended local public schools. He studied at the West Point U.S. Military Academy, graduating in 1915, and then served as a second lieutenant in the infantry, at Fort Sam Houston, Texas. During World War I, he served at various army posts, and in 1918 was training men at Camp Colt, Pennsylvania in the use of a new weapon - the tank. By 1926, he had graduated from Command and General Staff School, and in 1928 finished studies at Army War College. During the Depression, he worked with the Army's Chief of Staff in Washington, D.C., until 1935, when he was assigned to the Phillipines. In both assignments, he worked under *General Douglas MacArthur.* Eisenhower was made a brigadier general in 1941 as a result of his training performance with the Third Army. As the U.S. became involved in World War II, Eisenhower was hired to work in the War Plans Division, a highly important office in Washington. The next year (1942), he was made commander of the U.S. forces in Europe, and planned the crucial strategies of the Allies from London. His services were called for in North Africa later in 1942, and the next year he planned the invasion of Sicily and Italy. Before that invasion was completed, Eisenhower was called to command Operation Overload, which eventually resulted in D-Day (June 6, 1944), and the end of the War. He was made a permanent general in the Army in 1946, and was widely hailed as a hero in the United States. *President Truman* named him Army Chief of Staff in 1945, a seat which he retained until 1948, when he was appointed President of Columbia University. That same year, he published an account of his actions in World War II in the book, *Crusade in Europe.* It was a best-seller for many months. When the North

Atlantic Treaty Organization (NATO) was organized in 1950, Eisenhower again returned to his military activities as commander of that alliance. Determinedly against any communist or Soviet-inspired aggression in the world, he was a favorite with his fellow Republicans in this Cold War era. Although at first hesitant, Eisenhower agreed to run for President, and won by a large margin. In 1952, he resigned the Army and entered the Executive office, where he regarded his position as that of a moral leader. He concerned himself with foreign affairs more than domestic, and brought about an end to the Korean War by traveling to that country in mid-1953. He also advocated financial aid to sympathetic foreign countries in order to prevent Soviet takeover. Although he supported government aid to education and the elderly, *Eisenhower* mistrusted anything that hinted at what he called "creeping socialism," such as farm price supports and the Tennessee Valley Authority. He suffered a heart attack in 1955, but recovered enough to win the 1956 election. His policy of "modern Republicanism" and "dynamic conservatism" helped the Cold War between the U.S.S.R. and the U.S. to grow, and made room for the capricious attacks of *Senator Joseph McCarthy*. Eisenhower retired from office in 1960 to his farm near Gettysburg, Pennsylvania. The home is now a national historic site.

•EVANS, LEMUEL DALE, (1810-1877)- U. S. Representative, was born in Tennessee January 8; studied law and was admitted to the bar; moved to Marshall, Texas, in 1843 and engaged in the practice of law; member of the State convention that annexed the State of Texas to the Union in 1845; elected as the candidate of the American Party to the Thirty-fourth Congress (March 4, 1855-March 3, 1857); unsuccessful candidate for reelection in 1856 to the Thirty-fifth Congress; collector in internal revenue in 1867; member of the reconstruction convention in 1868; chief justice of the supreme court in 1870 and 1871; associate justice and presiding judge from 1872 to 1873, when he resigned; United States marshal for the eastern judicial district of Texas in 1875; died in Washington, D. C., on July 1.

F

•**FANNIN, JAMES W., JR.** (1800-1836), soldier, was born on a farm in North Carolina. He later moved to Georgia, and then in 1834 to Texas, where he worked on a plantation. Soon, Fannin was involved in the revolutionary movement among the Anglo-American colonists. He was made a captain under *James Bowie* and fought in the battle at the Mission of the Conception in 1835. Later that year, the provisional government and *General Sam Houston* named Fannin to the chief staff as a colonel, but Fannin declined the post because he was generally against the policies of *Governor Henry Smith* and *Houston*. However, a few months later he became an agent of the Republic government and was charged to command 500 men at Goliad in February, 1836. Fannin's plot to capture Matamoras on the Rio Grande failed after the Alamo occured, and *General Houston* ordered Fannin to move his men back to Victoria on the Guadalupe River. The young colonel did not begin to retreat for several days, however. Heavy fog shrouded the retreating soldiers for a few hours, but soon it became apparent that a Mexican force about equal to the Americans' had overtaken them. The Mexicans under *General Jose Urrea* soon surrounded them, and 60 of Fannin's men were killed or wounded on the first day (March 19). The next day, *Urrea's* troops had been reinforced by several hundred new men, and they soon captured the Texans. The wounded Fannin and his men were returned to the presidio at Goliad, and, under orders from *General Santa Anna*, were led out and executed. 500 men were killed in all.

•**FERGUSON, JAMES E.** (1871-1944), twenty-fifth governor of Texas (1915-17), was born in Temple, Bell County, Texas on his family's farm. His parents were *James Edward and Fannie Fitz-*

65

patrick Ferguson, who operated a grist mill on Salado Creek. Young James was only four when his father died, so he was not able to receive a formal education. When he was only 16, he left home to travel west, looking for work. He was a grape picker in California, a teamster on some large ranches, and a placer miner in the Rocky Mountains. He also worked in a San Francisco wire factory and a lumber cutter in Washington state before returning to Texas to work on construction of bridges. He also began to farm and study law; was admitted to the bar in 1897. Ferguson opened an office in Belton, Texas, and opened a small bank there as well. In Temple, Texas he organized another bank, which evolved into a major institution. He was campaign manager for *R. L. Henry* in 1902 and for *R. V. Davidson* in 1910. When he ran for governor in 1914 on an anti-prohibition platform, he won by one of the greatest majorities ever received by a gubernatorial candidate in Texas. He pushed for state aid to common schools and compulsory education in the state. He was reelected in 1916, but his popularity had waned. He was accused of misuse of state funds, and although the charges were acquitted, Ferguson continued to raise a storm when he attacked the University of Texas. Ferguson disliked several of the school's faculty members, and demanded their discharge. When university officials refused to do so, he tried to stop funding to the school. As a result, his opponents brought new charges against him, one of embezzlement of state funds. When he called a special session of the legislature to deal with the University of Texas, the meeting turned instead to a call for Ferguson's inpeachment. Instead, of waiting to be fired, Ferguson resigned his office, calling the proceedings against him a "kangaroo court." He tried again for the governorship in 1918, but his reputation had fallen greatly. He ran for President on the Know-Nothing ticket in 1920, and took a last stab at gaining political office in 1922 for U.S. Senator. After that, he concentrated on his wife's career, and helped her win the 1924 and 1932 gubernatorial elections. The two retired in 1940, at Austin, where he lived until his death there.

•FERGUSON, MIRIAM A. (1875-1961), twenty-eighth and thirty-first governor of Texas (1925-27 and 1933-35), was a native of Bell County Texas, the daughter of *Joseph L. and Eliza Garrison*

Wallace. She was educated at Salado (Texas) College and at Baylor College for Women, and led a quiet life after her marriage to *James E. Ferguson,* rearing her two daughters. She gained recognition when her husband became governor, and even more so after he was nearly impeached. He resigned instead, and Mrs. "Ma" Ferguson defended him in the next election, to no avail. In 1924, failing to get her husband's name on the ballot again, Mrs. Ferguson entered the contest herself. She was elected easily, and became the first woman governor of Texas, the second woman governor in U.S. history. Her platform had been anti-Ku Klux Klan, and one of her most important actions was to pass a law prohibiting the wearing of masks in public. She also succeeded in balancing the budget and sought enforcement of the state liquor law, being a staunch prohibitionist. She also differed from her husband in that she favored large appropriations for the University of Texas and all other state educational institutions. Governor Ferguson also granted large numbers of paroles, pardons and proclamations of clemency during her term, which gave her a kindly reputation. However, her husband's shadow followed her, and charges were soon made against her administration's use of funds. Political considerations, including the underlying trouble of the division of gubernatorial authority between an elected wife and her husband, and the influence of the Ku Klux Klan, led to her declining popularity. She lost her renomination for governor in 1926, and returned to political actions to clear her husband's reputation. However, Miriam was the favored Ferguson, and deep into the Great Depression, Texas voters returned to her again. Her second term was quiet, she maintained a conservative fiscal policy and continued to grant reprieves to worthy prisoners, going as far as to commute the sentences of several persons on Death Row. She did not seek reelection in 1934, but retired for a while in Austin. She did attempt a third term in 1940, but was defeated by *W. Lee Daniel.* When her husband died, Mrs. Ferguson lived privately in Austin until her death of a heart attack. She was buried next to her husband.

•FIELDS, JACK M, (1952-)- U. S. Representative, Republican, of Humble, Texas; was born in Humble, February 3; educated Humble Independent Schools, graduated, Humble High School,

1970; B.A., Baylor University, 1974; J.D., Baylor University Law School, 1977; vice president, Rosewood Memorial Funeral Home and Cemetery, a family-owned business; attorney in Humbel since 1977; school honors: student body president, Humble High School; student body president, Baylor University, junior and senior years; outstanding sophomore and senior man at Baylor University; listed in Who's Who in American Colleges and Universities in junior and senior years; current memberships include: trustee of Baylor University; executive board of Humble Northeast Medical Center; Humble Chamber of Commerce; Humble-Intercontinental Rotary and First Baptist Church of Humble; married in 1979 to the former Roni Sue Haddock; elected to 97th Congress, November 4, 1980; reelected to the 98th Congress, November 2, 1982.

•FISHER, O. CLARK, Democrat, of San Angelo, Texas; son of late Jobe and Rhoda Clark Fisher; born on sheep, goat, and cattle ranch in Kimble County; now engaged in that business; graduate of Junction (Texas) High School; attended Colorado, Texas, and Baylor Universities, with LL.B. from latter; married Marian DeWalsh; one daughter, Rhoda (Mrs. James W.) Grimes; 4 grandchildren, Stephen, Randal, Janet, and Cynthia; author of "It Occurred in Kimble," "Texas Heritage of Fishers and Clarks," "King Fisher," and joint author of "Great Western Indian Fights;" member, Sons of American Revolution and Sons of Republic of Texas; member of Masonic Order, Scottish Rite and Shrine; practiced law in San Angelo and served there as county attorney, State representative, and district attorney before being elected to 78th and succeeding Congresses; member Armed Services Committee; author of several laws creating major water conservation and flood control projects in his district; active cosponsor of many laws enhancing U.S. military strength.

•FLANAGAN, JAMES WINRIGHT, (1805-1887)- U. S. Senator, was born in Gordonsville, Orange County, Va., September 5; attended the common schools and received private instruction;

moved to Cloverport, Ky., in 1816, and engaged in mercantile pursuits; justice of the peace 1823-1833; studied law; was admitted to the bar in 1825 and practiced in the Breckenridge County circuit from 1833 to 1843; moved to Henderson, Rusk County, Texas, in 1843 and continued the practice of law; also engaged in mercantile and agricultural pursuits; member of the State house of representatives in 1851 and 1852; served in the State senate in 1855 and 1856; member of the State constitutional conventions in 1866 and 1868; elected Lieutenant Governor of Texas in 1869 and served until his resignation in 1870 to become Senator; upon the readmission of Texas to representation was elected as a Republican to the United States Senate and served from March 30, 1870, to March 3, 1875; was the caucus nominee of his party, which was in the minority in 1875; delegate to the Republican National Conventions at Philadelphia in 1872, at Cincinnati in 1876, and at Chicago in 1880; died in Longview, Gregg County, Texas, September 28.

•FROST, JONAS MARTIN, (1942-)- U. S. Representative, Democrat, of Dallas, Texas; was born in Glendale, California, January 1; attended the public schools; graduated R. L. Paschal High School, Fort Worth, Texas, 1960; B.A. and B.J., University of Missouri, Columbia, Mo., 1964; J.D., Georgetown Law Center, Washington, D.C., 1970; served in U.S. Army Reserve, 1966-72; lawyer; law clerk for Federal Judge Sarah T. Hughes; legal commentator for channel 13; vice president and board member, Dallas Democratic Forum, 1976-77; admitted to the Texas Bar in 1970 and commenced practice in Dallas, Texas; very active of Commerce, American Cancer Society, and Oak Cliff Conservation League; member: Oak Cliff Lions Club, American Jewish Committee, Temple Emanu-El in Dallas, Dallas and Texas Bar Associations; staff writer for the congressional Quarterly Weekly, 1965-67; married to the former Valerie Hall of Fort Worth, Texas, 1976; three daughters: Alanna, Mariel and Camille; elected to the 96th Congress, November 7, 1978; reelected to the 97th and 98th Congresses.

G

•GAMMAGE, ROBERT (BOB) ALTON, (1938-)- U. S. Representative, Democrat, of Houston, Texas; was born in Houston, Harris County, March 13; graduated, Milby High School, Houston, Texas, 1956; A.A., Del Mar College, Corpus Christi, Texas, 1958; B.S., University of Corpus Christi, 1963; M.A., Sam Houston State University, 1965; J.D., University of Texas School of Law, 1969; lawyer; admitted to the bar in 1969 and commenced practice in Houston; served in the U.S. Army, 1959-60; U.S. Army Reserve, 1960-64; U.S. Navy Reserve, 1965 to present; member, Texas House of Representatives, 1971-73; member, Texas Senate, 1973-76; member: American, Texas, and Houston Bar Associations; American Judicature Society; American and Texas Trial Lawyers Associations; Sierra Club; Houston Sportsmen's Club; and several other civic and professional organizations; designated one of the Outstanding Young Men of America for 1971 and 1973; received various other civic citations and awards; married to the former Judy Ann Adcock, 1962; three children: Terry Lynne, Sara Noel, and Robert Alton, Jr.; elected to the 95th Congress, November 2, 1976.

•GARNER, JOHN NANCE, (1868-1967)- U. S. Representative and a Vice President of the United States, was born near Detroit, Red River County, Texas, November 22; had limited elementary educational advantages; studied law in Clarksville, Texas; was admitted to the bar in 1890 and commenced practice in Uvalde, Uvalde County, Texas; judge of Uvalde County, Texas, 1893-1896; member of the State house of representatives 1898-1902; delegate to the Democratic National Conventions in 1900, 1916, and 1924; elected as a Democrat to the Fifty-eighth and to the fourteen succeeding Congresses (March 4, 1903-March 3, 1933); served as minority floor leader in the Seventy-first Congress and as Speaker in the Seventy-second Congress; reelected to the Seventy-third Congress on November 8, 1932, and on the same day was elected Vice President of the United States on the ticket headed by Franklin D. Roosevelt; resigned from the Seventy-third Congress on March 3, 1933; reelected Vice President in 1936 and served in that office from March 4, 1933, to January 20, 1941; retired to private life and resided in Uvalde, Texas, until his death there on November 7.

•GARRETT, CLYDE LEONARD, (1885-1959)- U. S. Representative, was born on a farm near Gorman, Eastland County, Texas; December 16; attended the public schools and Hankins' Normal College in his native city; raised on a farm; worked as a railroad section hand; taught school at Sweetwater, Nolan County, Texas, in 1906 and 1907; deputy in the office of the tax collector 1907-1912; county clerk of Eastland County, Texas, 1913-1919; engaged in the real estate, insurance, and banking businesses 1920-1922; city manager of the city of Eastland, Texas, in 1922 and 1923; county judge 1929-1936; elected as a Democrat to the Seventy-fifth and Seventy-sixth Congresses (January 3, 1937-January 3, 1941); unsuccessful candidate for renomination in 1940; administrative officer in the office of the Secretary of Commerce from January 15, 1941, to May 1, 1942, at which time he became staff specialist in the Office of War Information and served until October 15, 1943; unsuccessful candidate for Democratic nomination to the Seventy-ninth Congress in 1944; technical assistant, Veterans Administration, Washington, D. C., and Dallas, Texas., 1949-1950; manager, Veterans Administration regional office, Waco, Texas, from 1951 until retirement on January 1, 1956; was an unsuccessful candidate for Eastland County judgeship in 1958; died in Eastland, Texas, December 18.

•GARRETT, DANIEL EDWARD, (1869-1932)- U. S. Representative, born near Springfield, Robertson County, Tenn., April 28; attended the common schools of his native county; studied law;

was admitted to the bar and commenced practice in Springfield, Tenn., in 1893; member of the State house of representatives 1892-1896; elected to the State senate in 1902 and again in 1904; moved to Houston, Texas, in 1905 and continued the practice of law; elected as a Democrat to the Sixty-third Congress (March 4, 1913-March 3, 1915); unsuccessful candidate for reelection in 1914 to the Sixty-fourth Congress; resumed the practice of law in Houston, Texas; elected to the Sixty-fifth Congress (March 4, 1917-March 3, 1919); was not a candidate in renomination in 1918; elected to the Sixty-seventh and to the five succeeding Congresses and served from March 4, 1921, until his death; had been reelected to the Seventy-third Congress; died in Washington, D. C., on December 13.

•GENTRY, BRADY PRESTON, (1896-1966)- U. S. Representative, was born in Colfax, Van Zandt County, Texas, March 21; attended the public schools and East Texas State College, Commerce, Texas; graduated from Cumberland University, Lebanon, Tenn.; studied law; was admitted to the bar and began practice in Tyler, Texas; during the First World War enlisted in the United States Army in 1918; served in Europe and rose to the rank of captain of Infantry; was gassed during combat; discharged in 1919; county attorney of Smith County 1921-1924; county judge of Smith County 1931-1939; chairman of the Texaws State Highway Commission 1939-1945; elected as a Democrat to the Eighty-third and Eighty-fourth Congresses (January 3, 1953-January 3, 1957); was not a candidate for renomination in 1956 to the Eighty-fifth Congress; resumed the practice of law; died in Houston, Texas, November 9.

•GIBSON, WELDON BAILEY (1917-), research executive, was born on April 23, 1917 in Eldorado, Texas. He graduated from Washington State University in 1938 and received an MBA from Stanford in 1940. He served in the U.S. Air force from 1941 -46. After the war he worked as assistant director of the Air Force Institute of Technology, and director of economic research at Stanford Research Institute. Dr. Gibson has written a number of book: *Global Geography*, and *World Political Geography*. He is a member of the American Geographical Association, and the American Economics Association. Dr. Gibson is married and has one child.

•GIDDINGS, DE WITT CLINTON, (1827-1903), U. S. Representative, was born in Susquehanna County, Pa., July 18; pursued an academic course; studied law in Honesdale, Pa.; was admitted to the bar in Texas in 1852 and commenced practice in Brenham, Texas; served in the Confederate Army throughout the Civil War; member of the State constitutional convention 1866; successfully contested as a Democrat the election of William T. Clark to the Forty-second Congress;reelected to the Forty-third Congress and served from May 13, 1872, to March 3, 1875; again elected to the Forty-fifth Congress (March 4, 1877-March 3, 1879); engaged in the banking business in Brenham, Texas; delegate to the Democratic National Conventions in 1884, 1888, and 1892; died in Brenham, Texas on August 19.

•GILLESPIE, OSCAR WILLIAM, (1858-1927), U. S. Representative, was born near Quitman, Clarke County, Miss., June 20; attended private schools, and was graduated from Mansfield College, Texas in 1885; studied law; was admitted to the bar in 1886 and commenced practice in Fort Worth, Texas, assistant attorney of Tarrant County 1886-1888; prosecuting attorney of Tarrant County 1890-1894; elected as a Democrat to the Fifty-eighth and to the three succeeding Congresses (March 4, 1903-March 3, 1911); unsuccessful candidate for renomination in 1910; resumed the practice of law in Fort Worth, Texas, where he died August 23.

•GIRVIN, EB CARL (1917-), biologist and educator, was born on December 27, 1917 at Georgetown, Texas. He was educated at the University of Texas where he received a Masters Degreee in 1941. Dr. Girvin served in the USNR during World War II. After the war he earned a Ph.D, also at the University of Texas. From 1948 to 1953 he held an appointment as professor of biology at Millsap College. Subsquently Dr. Girvin became a professor of biology at Georgetown University. He has published extensively in professional journals. He is married and has three children.

•GONZALEZ, HENRY B., (1916-)- U. S. Representative, Democrat, of San Antonio, Texas; was born in San Antonio, May 3; son of Leonides (deceased) and Genevieve Gonzalez (deceased), descendants of the original colonists of the State of Durango in northern Mexico, who fled their country as the result of the revolution and moved to San Antonio in 1911; attended the San Antonio public schools, San Antonio College, University of Texas, and St. Mary's University School of Law (J.D. and LL.B) which conferred on him an honorary doctor of laws degree in 1965; honorary doctor of humanities degree, Our Lady of the Lake College, 1973; first elected to public office in 1953; served 3 years on the San Antonio City Council, serving as mayor pro tem part of the second term; served as chief probation officer of Bexar County Juvenile Court; worked for bilingual publications, San Antonio Housing Authority, and once taught math and citizenship classes in the veterans training program; elected to the State senate of Texas in 1956 and reelected in 1960; married Bertha Cuellar in 1940 and they have 4 boys and 4 girls; Henry, Rose Mary (Mrs. Jesus Ramos), Charles, Bertha (Mrs. Terry Denzer), Stephen, Genevieve (Mrs. Anthony Ruiz), Francis, and Anna Maria Solis and 13 grandchildren; elected to the 87th Congress on November 4, 1961, to fill the unexpired term of Paul J. Kilday; reelected to each succeeding Congress; member of the Banking, Finance and Urban Affairs Committee; chairman, Subcommittee on Housing and Community Development; member, Small Business Committee, previously served as chairman, ad hoc Subcommittee on Robinson-Patman Act, antitrust legislation, and related matters; member, Select Committee on the Missing in Action in Southeast Asia; House Select committee on Assassinations, vice chairman, 94th Congress; has served seven times as a House delegate to the U.S.-Mexico Interparliamentary Conference; member, National Commission on Consumer Finance (terminated December 1972); zone whip (Texas delegation), Majority Whip Organization.

•GOODNIGHT, CHARLES (1836-1929), cattle rancher, is famous for his one million acre ranch in West Texas. He was born in Macoupin County, Illinois, but moved at the age of 10 with his family to Milam County, Texas. By the time he was 20, Goodnight was in the cattle business which would eventually make him a fortune. He also joined the Texas Rangers and was a prominent Indian fighter. In 1857, he moved to Palo Pinto County and continued to work on cattle ranches. He joined in the Pease River battle with Indians under *Captain J.J. Cureton* in 1860, and when Civil War broke out he enlisted in the Frontier Regiment of the Texas Rangers. Goodnight became a noted guide and Indian scout in the Southwest during this time. In 1866, he purchased his first cattle ranch on the Pecos River in what is now New Mexico. Other ranches followed, in Colorado and Arkansas, Goodnight then saw that it was becoming increasingly necessary to begin a trail from the High Plains cattle ranges to the Northern markets. He laid out a trail from Belknap, Texas to Fort Sumner New Mexico in 1868 which has since been called the "Goodnight Trail." With *Oliver Loving*, he blazed another trail to Wyoming, called the "Goodnight-Loving Trail." More trails were established in the Western states before Goodnight decided to return to Texas in 1875. The economic climate was good for a pioneering cattleman: he brought 1,600 head of cattle aross 300 miles into Palo Duro Canyon. Soon, he began an alliance with wealthy Irishman *John Adair*, and established the J.A. Ranch. It became the largest in West Texas, with over 100,000 head of Shorthorns and Herefords-- the best beef cattle in America--on an endless range. Goodnight liked to experiment with breeding; he caught a few buffalo and crossed them with Angus cattle to produce "cattalos." The buffalos themselves went on to reproduce into a substantial herd, which helped in preventing them from going extinct. Indian fighting and battling with the outlaws of the region continued to be Charles Goodnight's favorite occupations, and he became a symbol for the Texas cattleman. He was large, fiesty, rough, and his legs were permanently bowed to fit around a saddle. He established an association for Panhandle ranchers around the turn of the century, and established schools in the area, including the Goodnight College (later taken over by the state). He married two times: in 1871 to *Mary Ann Dyer*, who died in 1926, and again in 1927 to *Corinne Goodnight*, who was not related in spite of her surname. His one child, from the second marriage, did not survive.

•**GOSSETT, ED LEE**, (1902-), U. S. Representative, was born in a sawmill camp known as Yellow Pine, near Many, Sabine Parish, La., January 27; moved to Texas in 1908 with his parents, who settled on a farm near Henrietta, Clay County; attended the rural schools of Clay and Garza Counties, Texas; University of Texas at Austin, A.B., 1924 and the law school of the same university, LL. B., 1927; was admitted to the bar the latter year and commenced practice in Vernon, Texas; moved to Wichita Falls, Texas, in 1937 and continued the practice of law; served as district attorney of the forty-sixth judicial district 1933-1937; elected as a Democrat to the Seventy-sixth and to the six succeeding Congresses and served from January 3, 1939, until his resignation July 31, 1951; resumed the practice of law and was general attorney for the Texas Southwestern Bell Telephone Co., presently serving as judge of Criminal District Court, Dallas, Texas, where he now resides.

•**GRAMM, WILLIAM PHILIP (PHIL)**, (1942-)- U. S. Representative, Democrat, of College Station, Texas; was born in Fort Benning, Ga., July 8; B.B.A., economics, 1964, Ph.D., economics, 1967, University of Georgia, Athens; named distinguished alumnus of College of Business Administration, University of Georgia, 1981; professor of economics, Texas A & M University, College Station, 1967-78; partner, Gramm and Associates, 1971-78; author of several books, including: "The Role of Government in a Free Society," 1982, and "The Economics of Mineral Extraction," 1980; articles in the American Economic Review, Journal of Money, Credit and Banking, and the Journal of Economic History, and guest editorials in the Wall Street Journal; special consultant on the environment and taxation, Ministry of Natural Resources, Province of Ontario, Canada, 1973-78; member: Gulf Universities Research Consortium, Energy Programs Planning Council, 1974-76; former consultant: U.S. Bureau of Mines, National Science Foundation, Arms Control and Disarmament Agency, U.S. Public Health Service; named one of five Outstanding Young Texans of 1977 by the Texas Jaycees; coauthor of the Gramm-Latta budget, mandating spending reductions totaling $143 billion in fiscal years 1982-84, adopted May 7, 1981; coauthor of the Gramm-Latta II Omnibus Reconciliation Act which changed existing law to reduce the level of expenditures for 250 Federal programs, lowering Federal outlays by a total of $131 billion in fiscal years 1982-84, signed into law August 13, 1981; author of the Safe Drinking Water Act amendments which limited the ability of the Environmental Protection Agency to impose regulations which would have been costly to water consumers and which would have limited oil and gas production, enacted December 5, 1980; married Dr. Wendy Lee, of Waialua, Hawaii, 1970; two children: Marshall Kenneth and Jefferson Philip; Episcopalian; member: Budget Committee, Energy and Commerce Committee (Subcommittees on Conservation and Power, Fossil and Synthetic Fuels, and Health and the Environment), and Veterans' Affairs Committee; elected to the 97th Congress, November 4, 1980; elected to the 98th Congress, November 2, 1982; resigned from the 98th Congress, as a Democrat, January 5, 1983; reelected to the 98th Congress, as a Republican, in a special election, February 12, 1983.

•GREGG, ALEXANDER WHITE, (1855-1919)- U. S. Representative, was born in Centerville, Leon County, Texas, January 31; attended the common schools of Texas, and was graduated from King College, Bristol, Tenn., in 1874; studied law at the University of Virginia at Charlottesville; was admitted to the bar in 1878 and commenced practice in Palestine, Texas; member of the State senate 1886-1888; resumed the practice of law; elected as a Democrat to the Fifty-eighth and to the seven succeeding Congresses (March 4, 1903-March 3, 1919); was not a candidate for renomination; died in Palestine, Anderson County, Texas, April 30.

•GRESHAM, WALTER, (1841-1920)- U. S. Representative, was born at "Woodlawn," near Newtown, King and Queen County, Va., July 22; attended Stevensville Academy and Edge Hill Academy, and was graduated from the University of Virginia at Charlottesville in 1863; served as a private in the Confederate Army during the Civil War; studied law; was admitted to the bar in 1867 and commenced practice in Galveston, Texas; district attorney for the Galveston judicial district in 1872; member of the

State house of representatives 1886-1891; elected as a Democrat to the Fifty-third Congress (March 4, 1893-March 3, 1895); unsuccessful candidate for reelection in 1894 to the Fifty-fourth Congress; resumed the practice of law in Galveston, Texas; died in Washington, D. C., November 6.

•GRIFFIN, JOHN HOWARD (1920-), author and photographer, was born June 16, 1920 in Dallas, Texas. Educated in France Mr. Griffin later received advanced degrees from Marycrest College. After service in the Air Force he worked for International News Service and King Features as a syndicated writer. He was a senior editor of *Ramparts* magazine, and the author of *Black Like Me*. Mr. Griffin published many stories and is included in numerous anthologies. He was awarded the Saturday Review Anisfield-Wolfe Prize , and the Pacem in Terris Award in 1964. Mr. Griffin is married and has three children.

•GROLLMAN, ARTHUR (1901-), Physician and Scientist, was born October 20, 1901 in Baltimore, Maryland. He was educated at Johns Hopkins receiving both a Ph.D and an M.D. there in 1930. After graduation he worked as a medical researcher at Johns Hopkins, University of London, University of Berlin, and the University of Heidelberg. Dr. Grollman had many appointments including professor of medicine at Southwestern College, professor of pharmacology at Baylor University, and the Bowman Gray School of Medicine in Winston-Salem, N.C. He has written over ten books and 350 scientific articles for professional journals. He served as a consultant to the USPHS and the Surgeon General. Dr. Grollman was a member of the AMA, and a fellow of the American College of Physicians. He was married and the father of three children.

•GUILL, BEN HUGH, (1909-)- U. S. Representative, was born in Smyrna, Rutherford County, Tenn., September 8; moved to Hereford, Deaf Smith County, Texas, in 1918; attended the public schools of Hereford, El Paso, and Canyon, Texas; was graduated from West Texas State College at Canyon in 1933; taught in the public schools of Amarillo, Pampa, Panhandle, and Hopkins, Texas, 1929-1936; president of the Royal Crown Bottling Co., Amarillo, Texas, 1939-1942; during World War II served in the United States Navy as a lieutenant commander 1942-1945; engaged in seven amphibious landings on shore gunnery control duty and was wounded in action; awarded Bronze Star and Purple Heart Medal; returned to Pampa, Texas, in september 1945 and engaged in the real-estate business; elected as a Republican to the Eighty-first Congress to fill the vacancy caused by the resignation of Eugene Worley, and served from May 6, 1950, to January 3, 1951; unsuccessful candidate for reelection in 1950 to the Eighty-second Congress; delegate to Republican National Convention in 1952; executive assistant to the Postmaster General, Washington, D. C., from February 1953 to January 1955; was appointed a member of the Federal Maritime Board in 1955; reappointed in 1957 and served as vice chairman until his resignation December 31, 1959; engaged as a public relations consultant; resides in Washington, D. C.

•GUTIERREZ, JOSE ANGEL (1944-), Chicano leader in the Southwest, mainly in Texas. He was born in Crystal City, Texas and later graduated with a degree in political science from Texas A & I University. At the time he received the degree in 1965, he had become aware of the underrepresentation of Mexican-Americans in Texas politics, even in places where they dominated the population. To combat the established order of things, he formed a new political party, La Raza Unida ("United People") with the purpose of bringing more Chicanos into politics. The organization now spread throughout the south and midwestern United States nominates Mexican-American candidates for office. Gutierrez himself was elected to the Crystal City school board in 1970 as a result of a Raza nomination and campaign. In this position, he helped bring bilingual education into the local classrooms. La Raza Unida subsequently sponsored successful campaigns for city and local elections in several states. Since his school board days, Gutierrez has received a degree in political science from the University of Texas at Austin (1976). Since 1975, he has also been a county judge for Zavala County, Texas. He is the author of several articles and one book on Chicano rights.

H

•**HALL, RALPH MOODY,** (1923-)- U. S. Representative, Democrat, of Rockwall, Texas; was born in Fate, May 3; attended Fate and Rockwall public schools; graduated, Rockwall High School, 1941; attended Texas Christian University, University of Texas, and received LL.B., Southern Methodist University, 1951; lieutenant (senior grade), U.S. Navy, carrier pilot, 1942-45; lawyer; admitted to the Texas Bar in 1951 and commenced practice in Rockwall; former president and chief executive officer, Texas Aluminum Corp.; general counsel, Texas Extrusion Co., Inc.; director, First State Bank of Rockwall; founding chairman and board member, Lakeside National Bank of Rockwall; owner-president of North Texas Grain & Elevator Co., Inc.; chairman, Lakeside News, Inc.; county judge, Rockwall County, 1950-62; member, Texas State Senate, 1962-72; member: First Methodist Church; American Legion Post 117; VFW Post 6796; Rockwall Rotary Club; married to the former Mary Ellen Murphy, 1944; three sons: Hampton, Brett, and Blakeley; elected to the 97th Congress, November 4, 1980; reelected to the 98th Congress.

•**HALL, SAM BLAKELEY, JR.** (-), U.S. Representative from Texas, was born in Marshall, Texas, the son of Judge and Mrs. Sam B. Hall. He graduated from Marshall High School in 1940 and entered the College of Marshall (now East Texas Baptist College. He attended the University of Texas Law School from 1942-43, but left to enter the U.S. Air Force where he served from 1943-45. On his return, he entere Baylor University Law School and graduated with an LL.B. degree in 1948. He was admitted to the bar the same year and began practice in Marshall, Texas. He continued his law practice in Marshall until 1976 when he was elected to Congress in a special election, to fill the vacancy caused by the death of Wright Patman. He has been reelected to each succeeding Congress.

Hall twice received Marshall's Outstanding Citizen Award. In 1946 he married Madeleine Segal. They have three children: Linda Rebecca, Amanda Jane, and Sandra Blake Hall.

•HAMILTON, ANDREW JACKSON (1815-1875), tenth governor of Texas (1865-66), was born in Huntsville, Alabama to *James and Abigail Bayless Hamilton*. After studying law, he moved to La Grange, Texas in 1846 and gained a reputation at the bar so that he was appointed attorney-general of Texas by *Governor Bell* (1849). He was elected in 1851 and 1853 to the state legislature as a Democrat, and to Congress in 1859 as an Independent. A strong Unionist, Hamilton stayed in Washington after his southern colleagues seceded and left. When he returned to Texas, he was elected to the state legislature on the Union ticket, but refused to take a seat under the Confederate government. He was soon regarded as a traitor in his own state, and so had to escape through Mexico to the North and to Washington, D.C. where *President Lincoln* made him brigadier general of the Federal Texas troops, a position he never exercised. In July 1865 he returned to Texas triumphantly with Federal troops, as *Andrew Johnson* had appointed him provisional governor to carry out his reconstruction policies. He fulfilled the onerous duties of this position as well as he could, advising former slaves to continue to work for their former masters at moderate wages in order to prove themselves worthy of freedom. Hamilton also authorized a new state constitution, rescinding the acts of secession and repudiating the Confederates' war debts. It also allowed for a division of Texas into one or more new states. The new constitution was ratified in 1866, but Hamilton was not reelected later that year, so he retired to his home to practice law. Shortly after, he was appointed an associate justice to the state supreme court and was active in Loyalist and Conservative activities until his death at Austin.

•HAMILTON, MORGAN CALVIN, (1809-1893)- (brother of Andrew Jackson Hamilton) (U. S. Senator, was born near Huntsville, Madison County, Ala., February 25; attended the public schools; engaged in mercantile pursuits in Elyton, Ala.; moved to the Republic of Texas in 1837; clerk in the War Department of the Republic of Texas 1839-1845 and acted as Secretary of War and Marine ad interim of that Republic from December 9, 1844, to March 10, 1845; appointed comptroller of the treasury of Texas in 1867; delegate to the State constitutional convention in 1868; upon the readmission of the State of Texas to representation was elected on February 22, 1870, as a Republican to the United States Senate to fill the vacancy in the term ending March 3, 1871; subsequently elected for the term commencing March 4, 1871, and served from March 30, 1870, to March 3, 1877; retired from public life and traveled extensively; was a resident of Brooklyn, N.Y., until his death; died in San Diego, Calif., where he had been visiting, November 21.

•HANCE, KENT R, (1942-)- U. S. Representative, Democrat, of Lubbock, Texas; was born in Dimmitt, November 14; attended the public schools; graduated from Dimmitt High School, 1961; B.B.A., Texas Tech University, 1965; LL.B., University of Texas School of Law, 1968; admitted to the Texas Bar in 1968 and commenced practice in Lubbock, Texas; lawyer; professor, Texas Tech University, 1968-73; member, Texas Senate, 1974-79; served on the board of regents, West Texas State University, 1972-74; one of the original incorporators of the Texas Boys' Ranch at Lubbock; member: Texas and American Bar Associations; Southwest Rotary Club; Lubbock Lions; First Baptist Church; Chamber of Commerce; Texas Tech Century Club; Water, Inc.; board of trustees, Wayland Baptist University; married to the former Carol Hays of Dimmitt, 1964; two children: Ron and Susan; elected to the 96th Congress, November 7, 1978; reelected to the 97th and 98th Congresses.

•HANCOCK, JOHN, (1824-1893)- U. S. Representative, was born near Bellefonte, Jackson County, Ala., October 24; attended the public schools and the University of Tennessee at Knoxville; studied law; was admitted to the bar in 1846; settled in Austin, Texas, in 1847 and practiced his profession there until August

1851; served as judge of the second judicial district of Texas from 1851 to 1855, when he resigned; resumed the practice of law and engaged in planting and stock raising; member of the State house of representataives in 1860 and 1861; refused to take the oath of allegiance to the Confederate States and was expelled from the legislature; took up his residence in the North until the conclusion of the war, when he returned to Texas; member of the State constitutional convention in 1866; elected as a Democrat to the Forty-second, Forty-third, and Forty-fourth Congresses (March 4, 1871 -March 3, 1877); unsuccessful candidate for renomination; elected to the Forty-eighth Congress (March 4, 1883-March 3, 1885); was not a candidate for renomination; resumed the practice of law; died in Austin, Texas, July 19.

•HARDIN, JOHN WESLEY (1853-95), considered the most famous gunfighter in the West, was born to a Methodist preacher's family in Bonham, Texas. At the age of 15, he killed a black man in a fight and was forced to hide from the law. His intense loyalty to the South and his hatred of the freed slaves caused him to kill four other black men during the Reconstruction, as well as many Union soldiers who happened to cross his path. In May 1874, he shot Deputy Sheriff *Charles Webb* of Brown County, which made him a fugitive for three years as well as a prisoner for a lengthy term in the Huntsville State Prison. While there, he became an avid reader, especially of the Bible. Although he spent some time aspiring to the ministry, he abandoned it for the study of law. But even these plans were crushed when his wife died. Although he passed the bar examination he turned away from the courts and tried unsuccessfully for the sheriff's seat in Gonzales, Texas. He retired for a time in a small town, but was called to help a distant relative, *"Killin' Jim" Miller* of Pecos, who wanted Hardin to prosecute for him in a case against one of his assailants. The trial took place in El Paso, and ended in a hung jury. However, he stayed in town and became involved with the wife of a cattle stealer when he agreed to defend him. The case was settled when the cattle stealer was shot in a duel.

A few months later, Hardin himself was shot by a gunfighter, *John Selman*, in a bar after he insulted *Selman's* son several times.

•**HARDY, RUFUS,** (1855-1943)- U. S. Representative, was born near Aberdeen, Monroe County, Miss., December 16; attended private schools in Texas and Somerville Institute in Mississippi; was graduated from the law department of the University of Georgia at Athens in 1875; was admitted to the bar the same year and commenced practice in Navasota, Texas; moved to Corsicana, Navarro County, Texas, in 1878; prosecuting attorney of Navarro County 1880-1884; district attorney for the thirteenth judicial district 1884-1888; district judge from 1888 to December 1896, when he retired; chairman of the Texas Sound Money Democracy in 1896; resumed the practice of law in Corsicana, Texas; elected as a Democrat to the Sixtieth and to the seven succeeding Congresses (March 4, 1907-March 3, 1923); was not a candidate for renomination in 1922; resumed the practice of his profession; died in Corsicana, Texas, March 13.

•**HARE, SILAS,** (1827-1907)- U. S. Representative, was born in Ross County, Ohio, November 13; moved to Hamilton County, Ind., in 1840 with his parents, who settled near Noblesville; attended the common and private schools; served during the war with Mexico as a private in Captain Drake's company, First Regiment, Indiana Volunteers, 1846 and 1847; studied law; was admitted to the bar in 1850 and commenced practice in Noblesville, Ind.; moved to Belton, Texas, in 1853 and continued the practice of law; chief justice of New Mexico in 1862 under the Confederate Government; during the Civil War served as a captain in the Confederate Army; settled in Sherman, Texas, in 1865 and resumed the practice of law; district judge of the criminal court 1873-1876; delegate to the Democratic National Convention at Chicago in 1884; presidential elector for the State at large on the Democratic ticket of Cleveland and Hendricks in 1884; elected as a Democrat to the Fiftieth and Fifty-first Congresses (March 4, 1887-March 3, 1891); unsuccessful candidate for renomination in 1890; resumed the practice of law in Washington, D.C., where he died November 26.

•HAWLEY, ROBERT BRADLEY, (1849-1921)- U. S. Representative, was born in Memphis, Tenn., October 25; attended the public schools and the Christian Brothers' College, Memphis, Tenn.; moved to Galveston, Texas, in 1875; was a merchant, importer, and manufacturer in the city of Galveston for twenty years; president of the Galveston Board of Education 1889-1893; temporary chairman of the Republican State convention at San Antonio September 4, 1890; delegate to several Republican National Conventions; elected as a Republican to the Fifty-fifth and Fifty-sixth Congresses (March 4, 1897-March 3, 1901); was not a candidate for renomination in 1900; organized and became president of the Cuban-American Sugar Co. in 1900; died in New York City November 28.

•HAYS, JOHN C. "JACK" (1817-1883), Indian fighter, was known for his knowledge of the frontier and his organization of the Texas Rangers. He was born in Wilson County, Tennessee, where he learned surveying. He moved to Mississippi and then continued working as a surveyor, but became more active as an Indian fighter, especially when he joined the Texas Republic Army as a scout. At that time, the Texas Rangers were a loosely allied group of men who took it upon themselves to push Indians out of the lands needed for white settlement in Texas. Hays trained his own regiment, which became strikingly more organized and skillful then the other Ranger groups. He fought in the Battle of Salado in 1842 against a Mexican army, and then commanded the advance company of the Somervell expedition against Mexico in the same year. In 1844, he and his 16 men fought successfully against 70 Comanche warriors. Many attributed the victory to the Rangers' cool-headedness and strong military skill, as well as the Jack Hays new "six-shooter" gun. Hays became a colonel of the volunteer Texas Cavalry during the Mexican War, commanding a regiment under *General Zachary Taylor* in 1846. He won national fame for this fearlessness at the storming of Monterrey, Mexico. When the war was over, Hays moved to California. In 1850, he was elected the first sheriff of San Francisco. He was also the state surveyor-general for many years until he returned to the strength of his investment income. Hays died at home in Piedmont, California.

•HEMPHILL, JOHN, (1803-1862)- (uncle of John James Hemphill and great-great-uncle of Robert Witherspoon Hemphill)- U. S. Senator, was born in Chester District, S. C., December 18; was graduated from Jefferson College in 1825; studied law; was admitted to the bar in 1829 and commenced practice in Sumter, S. C.; edited a nullification paper in 1832 and 1833; second lieutenant in the war with the Seminole Indians in 1836; moved to Texas in 1838; elected judge of the fourth judicial district of Texas in 1840 and served until 1842, when he resigned; adjutant general in the Mier expedition in 1842; chief justice of the supreme court of Texas 1846-1858; elected as a State Rights Democrat to the United States Senate and served from March 4, 1859, until expelled by resolution of July 11, 1861; he was one of the fourteen Senators who met on January 6, 1861, and recommended immediate secession of their States; deputy in the Provisional Congress of the Confederacy in Montgomery, Ala., in 1861; died in Richmond, Va., January 7.

•HENDERSON, JAMES PINCKNEY, (1808-1858)- U. S. Senator, was born in Lincolnton, Lincoln County, N. C., March 31; pursued academic studies in Lincolnton; was graduated from the University of North Carolina at Chapel Hill; served as side-de-camp to Major General Dorrett of the Carolina Militia in 1830 and subsequently was elected colonel; studied law; was admitted to the bar in 1828 and commenced practice in Lincolnton, N. C.; moved to Mississippi in 1835 and recruited a company for service in behalf of the Republic of Texas; preceded his company to Austin, Texas, in 1836; was commissioned brigadier general and returned to the United States to recruit volunteers; raised a company at his own expense; appointed by President Houston as Attorney General of the Republic of Texas in 1836, and as Secretary of State in 1837; visited Europe as the diplomatic representative of the Republic of Texas in 1838, and in 1844 visited the United States as special minister to negotiate annexation; member of the State constitutional convention in 1845; elected as the first Governor of the State of Texas in 1846; commissioned major general in the United States Army and served in the Mexican War; received from Congress a vote of thanks and a sword for bravery in action; completed his term of office as Governor; declined to be a candidate for reelection; appointed as a State Rights Democrat to the United States Senate to fill the vacancy caused by the death of Thomas J. Rusk and served from November 9, 1857, until his death in Washington, D. C., June 4.

•HENRY, ROBERT LEE, (1864-1931)- (great-great-great-grandson of Patrick Henry)(1736-1799)- U. S. Representative, was born in Linden, Cass County, Texas, May 12; attended the common schools; moved to Bowie County in 1878 and to McLennan County in 1895; was graduated from the Southwestern University of Texas at Georgetown in 1885; studied law; was admitted to the bar in 1886 and practiced for a short time in Texarkkna, Texas; was graduated from the University of Texas at Austin in 1887; elected mayor of Texarkana in 1890 but resigned in 1891; first office assistant to the attorney general of Texas 1891-1893; assistant attorney general 1893-1896; settled in Waco, McLennan County, Texas, in 1895 and practiced law; elected as a Democrat to the Fifty-fifth and to the nine succeeding Congresses (March 4, 1897-March 3, 1917); was not a candidate for renomination in 1916, but was an unsuccessful candidate for the Democratic nomination for United States Senator; engaged in the practice of law in Waco, Texas; again an unsuccessful candidate for the Democratic nomination for United States Senator in 1922 and 1928; moved to Houston, Texas, in 1923 and resumed the practice of his profession; died in Houston, Texas, July 9.

•HIGHTOWER, JACK ENGLISH, (1926-)- U. S. Representative, Democrat, of Vernon, Texas; was born in Memphis, Hall County, September 6; graduate, Memphis High School, 1944; Baylor University, Waco, Texas, B.A., 1949; LL.B., 1951; LL.D., Howard Payne College, 1971; served in U.S. Navy, 1944-46; Texas House of Representatives, 1953-54; district attorney, 1955-61; former member: Texas Law Enforcement Study Commission, 1957; served as president, Texas District and County Attorneys Association; vice president, Texas Junior Bar Association; board of regents, Midwestern University, Wichita Falls, Texas,

1962-64; Texas Senate, 1965-74; former member board of directors, Baptist Standard, Executive Board and Human Welfare Commission of the Baptist General Convention of Texas; former member board of trustees, Baylor University, 1972-81; member: Lions; American Legion; Distinguished Alumnus, 1978; Phi Alpha Delta Outstanding Alumni Award, 1972; Grand Master of Masons in Texas, 1972; married to the former Colleen Ward of Tulia, Texas; three daughters: Ann, Amy, and Alison; elected to the 94th Congress, November 5, 1974; reelected to each succeeding Congress.

•HOBBY, WILLIAM P. (1878-1964), twenty-sixth governor of Texas (1917-21) was born in Moscow, Texas, the son of *Edwin E. and Eudora Pettus Hobby.* He attended Houston High School and studied with private tutors until he was 17 and became a reporter with the Houston *Post.* In 1905, he was made managing editor of that newspaper; two years later he owned two papers himself in Beaumont, which he managed until 1930. In 1916-17, he was director of the Federal Land Bank of Houston. Early on, he also became an active Democrat and had been elected lieutenant governor under *James Ferguson* in 1914 and 1916. When *Ferguson* resigned, Hobby automatically became governor. He was elected in his own right in 1918 for a full term. As war governor of Texas, Hobby immediately enacted special military measures to support the federal government. He was forced to declare martial law and occupy the port of Galveston when strikers kept freighters from unloading there. He also provided for relief of drought victims in western Texas as well as those whose possessions were lost in hurricanes in Corpus Christi. He approved spending limits on political campaigns and increased the state highways budget. Hobby left office to become president of the Houston *Post,* and in 1924 brought about a merger between that paper and the *Dispatch.* He also built up the circulation from 35,855 in 1921 to 155,317 in 1946. In 1939, he and his wife, *Oveta Culp Hobby* had purchased the *Post-Dispatch.* He also continued to own the Beaumont papers until 1930, and in the 1950s he acquired Houston's KPRC radio station as well as KPRC-TV. Hobby died and was buried in his hometown.

•HOGG, JAMES STEPHEN (1851-1906), nineteenth governor of Texas (1891-95), was born at his family estate, "Mountain Home", near Rusk, Texas. He was the son of *Joseph Lewis*, a rancher and Texas legislator, and *Lucanda McMath Hogg*. The family was of Irish descent, and Hogg was the first governor to be born in Texas. His father died during the Civil War, however, and young James was obliged to find a job to support himself and the family, whose fortunes were depleted during the Reconstruction. He had been privately tutored and in 1866 attended school near Tuscaloosa, Alabama before returning to Texas to complete his education. He entered a printing office at the age of 16 and with his savings opened a plant that printed newspapers. In 1871 he established a paper called *The News* at Longview, Texas. Within a year he moved to Quitman and continued his paper until 1873, when he was elected justice of the peace (he had studied law on the side) of his home county. He was elected county attorney in 1878, and when that term was over he was elected district attorney, being reelected in 1882. Hogg had married *Sallie Stinson* in 1874 and became the father of four children. Having been admitted to the bar, he was able to practice law after 1886. After that, he resided in Austin and was elected governor in 1890, defeating the Republican candidate by hundreds of thousands of votes. He established the Texas Railroad Commission while in office, and presided over acts that limited corporate powers. He was elected to a second term, but declined to run for a third. Afterwards, he formed the law firm of Hogg, Watkins and Jones in Houston, but didn't actively engage in politics again. Hogg built up the family fortune again in the late 1890s when oil was discovered on his land. He died at Houston, but was buried in Austin.

•HOLLOWAY, WILLIAM VERNON (1903-), educator, was born in Weimer, Texas on October 18, 1903. He was educated at Southwestern University, University of Wisconsin, and the University of Washington. He received a Ph.D in political science in 1932. Over his career Dr. Holloway was professor of political science at the University of Alabama, Tulane, and the Universtiy of Tulsa. He was a member of the American Political Science Association, and author of several books on various aspects of American government. He was married and had two children.

•HOLLY, BUDDY (1936-1959), early rock and roll singer-composer, was born in Lubbock, Texas, into a religious family which encouraged music appreciation. Holley (his name was later altered in a recording contract), studied piano and violin, and then took up the steel guitar, a classic country and western instrument. Next, he began playing an acoustic guitar, imitating his favorite singers, such as *Hank Williams* and *Jimmie Rodgers*. While attending junior high school, he met *Bob Montgomery*, with whom he began to perform at school dances and local radio shows. Between 1950 and 1952, the duo were the most popular performers in Lubbock, and by the time they entered high school, they had performed as far away as New Mexico and Amarillo, Texas. In 1955, they were an opening act for Bill Haley and the Comets when that group performed in Lubbock. A talent scout from Decca Records heard a demonstration tape of the "Buddy and Bob" group in 1956, and invited Holley to Nashville for his first recording of such songs as "Blue Days Black Nights," and "Modern Don Juan". These recordings did not sell well, however, and Holley returned to Lubbock to record on his own crude equipment in his garage. He recorded "That'll Be the Day" at a small studio in Clovis, New Mexico, and in June, 1957, it was released by Brunswick Records. Within three months, it was a number one hit in both the U.S. and England. Buddy Holly (his new name) and the Crickets continued to record and perform such songs as "Oh Boy!", "Peggy Sue," and "Maybe Baby" in the next few years. The group toured the United States, Great Britain and Australia between 1957 and 1958. In the meantime, Holly married *Maria Elena Santago*, who worked as a secretary at Peer-Southern Organization, which published his music. The Hollys moved into an apartment in New York, and soon the rest of the Crickets decided to make that city their home base as well. However, Holly began to work more and more on his own. He spent three months in late 1958 recording songs such as "Raining in My Heart," and "It Doesn't Matter Anymore," which later became hits. By January 1959, Holly had broken up with the Crickets and began a tour with other rock and roll singers in what was called "The Biggest Show of the Stars of 1959." However, the tour stopped short in February 2, 1959, when the small plane Holly and two other popular singers had been riding in to Minnesota crashed in an Iowa cornfield. As with many artists who die in their prime, Holly's music became more popular after the tragic accident. The 1972 *Don McLean* song, "The Day the Music Died," commemorates the short career of Holly, as does the mid-1970s film, "The Buddy Holly Story."

•HOUSTON, ANDREW JACKSON (1854-1941) (son of Samuel Houston)- U. S. Senator, was born in Independence, Washington County, Texas, June 21; attended the common schools, Baylor University, Waco, Texas, Bastrop (Texas) Military Academy, Texas Military Institute at Austin, and Old Salado (Texas) College; appointed to West Point (N.Y.) Military Academy in June 1871 and was honorably discharged due to physical disability in 1873; employed as a clerk in the State school department 1873-1875 and in the General Land Office, Washington, D. C., in 1875; one of the organizers of the Travis Rifles at Austin during the reconstruction period in 1874; studied law; was admitted to the bar on April 21, 1876, and practiced in Tyler, Texas, 1876-1879; clerk of the United States district court at Dallas, Texas, 1879-1889; served in the Texas National Guard 1884-1893 with the rank of colonel; practiced law in Dallas, Texas, 1889-1901 and in Beaumont, Texas, in 1901 and 1902; during the Spanish american War formed a troop of Cavalry for the Rough Riders of Theodore Roosevelt but was not a member thereof; appointed United States marshal for the eastern district of Texas at Beaumont by President Theodore Roosevelt and served from 1902 to 1910; unsuccessful Prohibition Party candidate for Governor of Texas in 1910 and 1912; professor of military science and tactics at St. Mary's University in 1917 and 1918; retired from active business pursuits in 1918 and lived near La Porte, Texas, and was engaged as a writer and author; appointed by Governor Neff in 1924 as superintendent of the State park at the San Jacinto battleground and served until appointed to the Senate; appointed as a Democrat to the United States Senate to fill the vacancy in the term ending January 3, 1943, caused by the death of Morris Sheppard and served from April 21, 1941, until his death; died in a hospital in Baltimore, Md., June 26.

•**HOUSTON, SAMUEL** (1793-1863), first and third president of the Republic of Texas (1836-38, 1841-44), and sixth governor of Texas (1859-61), after being seventh governor of Tennessee (1827-28), was born in Timber Ridge Church in Rockbridge County, Virginia. His parents were *Samuel and Elizabeth Paxton Houston*, who had nine children altogether and owned a plantation. His father died when he was 13, and his mother moved the family to Blount County Tennessee, where he continued his education at local county schools. His neighbors were Cherokee people, and young Sam befriended the chief *Oolooteka* and learned the ways and customs of the tribe. He also learned their difficult language and began to prefer the freer and more natural lifestyle of the Indians. At the age of 18, however, he began teaching at a local school and later studied at an academy before enlisting in the U.S. Army to fight in the Creek War. Under *General Andrew Jackson*, he soon was promoted to sergeant, ensign, and then to second lieutenant. He was wounded in the Battle of Horseshoe Bend, but that did not stop him from attaining first lieutenancy in the army in 1818. However, accusations by the War Department that he was smuggling black slaves from Florida into the U.S. caused him to resign his post and go to Nashville to learn the law. He was elected district attorney there in 1819 and soon served as adjutant general and the major general of Tennessee. He served as a U.S. congressman from Tennessee in 1923-27, aligning with *Andrew Jackson* as a Democrat. On returning to Tennessee, he was elected governor but declined reelection. In 1929 he had married *Eliza H. Allen*, but the marriage failed, and when he resigned the governorship later that year, he moved to Indian territory and settled at Fort Gibson. The public was amazed at his sudden disappearance, and it was not discovered until after Houston's death that the reason he and *Eliza* separated was because of her love for another man. The two later obtained a legal divorce from the Republic of Texas (1833). Houston lived with the Cherokees for three years, taking the name Colonneh, and even fighting for the Indian cause in Washington in 1830. He was appointed an agent for the Indians by *President Jackson*, which pleased the Cherokees. Houston was not a man to mince words, and was often in trouble for his battleground inclinations. He had seriously wounded a *General William White* of Nashville in a duel in 1826, and while he was an

Indian agent in 1832 he fought on a street in Washington with a Congressman who claimed he was furnishing supplies to the Indians by a fraudulent contract. For his actions, the House voted to give Houston a mild reprimand and to fine him $500, although *President Jackson* paid the bill. While living among the Indians, Houston fell in love with a woman named *Tyania Rodgers*, half Cherokee, with whom he lived in common law marriage from 1830 until his return to white society in 1832. Secretly, he had been planning to overthrow the Mexican authority in Texas, and with a few companions he set out for Nacogdoches, Texas where he was cordially received by both American colonists and the Mexican authorities. In April 1833, he joined a convention at San Felipe de Austin, and drafted the constitution for the proposed state of Texas. Mexican authorities, concerned with their own governmental problems, disregarded the convention, but Houston received growing recognition as the leader of a revolutionary movement. American colonists were angered over taxes as well as the abolishment of slavery under the Mexican government. In 1836, Houston signed the Declaration of Independence from Mexico, and the Revolution began. Houston was able to defeat Mexican *General Santa Anna* in the Battle of San Jacinto by confusing him and spreading the Mexican army too thin to fight effectively against his men. He became the first regular president of the new Republic in late 1936, and after his 26 month term was a member of the Texas Congress. In 1841, he was once again President of Texas, with the task of reorganizing the government that had nearly dissolved under his predecessor. When Texas entered the United States as no state had before, Houston was elected to the U.S. Senate and served 14 years in Washington. Houston joined the "Know-Nothing" party and was considered for Presidential nomination in 1856. He tried unsuccessfully for Texas governorship in 1857 because he believed that Congress had a right to legislate regarding slavery in its territories, which was in opposition to the prevailing Southern sentiment. However, in 1859 he was favored once again and elected to the governorship. Houston, uncharacteristically for a Southerner, opposed the growing secessionist movement in Texas. Houston had also become seriously religious when he married his third wife, *Margaret Lea* in 1840, and joined the Baptist church. Because he was opposed to seceding from the Union, he was not nominated in 1860 when he sought the presidency again. In 1861, he refused to take an oath of allegiance to the new Confederate state and was forced out of office. The Revolutionary general retired to his farm with his wife and eight children at Huntsville, Texas, where he died.

•**HOWARD, VOLNEY ERSKINE,** (1809-1889)- U. S. Representative, was born in Norridgewock, Somerset County, Maine, October 22; completed preparatory studies; attended Bloomfield Academy and Waterville College; studied law; was admitted to the bar in 1832 and commenced practice in Brandon, Miss.; member of the State house of representatives in 1836; chosen by the legislature to carry the electoral vote for Van Buren to Washington, D. C.; reporter of the supreme court of the State of Mississippi; unsuccessful Democratic candidate for election in 1840 to the Twenty-seventh Congress; editor of the Mississippian; fought duels with Sergeant S. Prentiss and Alexander G. McNutt; moved to New Orleans, La., and was admitted to the bar there; moved to San Antonio, Texas; in 1847; member of the first State constitutional convention; elected as a Democrat to the Thirty-first and Thirty-second Congresses (March 4, 1849-March 3, 1853); unsuccessful candidate for reelection in 1852 to the Thirty-third Congress; sent on a special mission to California by the President; resigned, and engaged in the practice of law in San Francisco, Calif.; moved to Los Angeles in 1861 and continued the practice of law; district attorney 1861-1870; declined the nomination for judge of the supreme court; delegate to the State constitutional convention in 1878 and 1879; elected judge of the superior court of Los Angeles in 1879; retired at the end of one term on account of ill health; died in Santa Monica, Calif., May 14.

•**HUBBARD, RICHARD B.** (1834-1901), fifteenth governor of Texas (1876-79), was born in Walton County, Georgia to *Richard B. and Serena Cartor Hubbard.* After his common school education, young Richard studied at Mercer University in Macon, Georgia, and at Harvard Law School, completing his studies when he was only 21. He moved immediately to Tyler, Texas where he began practicing law. He was on the side of the Confederates during the Civil War, raised a regiment, was promoted to Colonel by the time of the South's defeat. Before that, he had served as a U.S. district attorney for West Texas, and was a member of the state House of Representatives. After the war, he was a Democrat who for a while was on the outside of Republican Reconstructionist politics. In 1873, he was elected lieutenant governor of Texas, and when Governor Coke resigned to join the U.S. Senate, he automatically stepped up to fill the unexpired term. The new constitution had changed the length of the governors' official tenure and so Coke was not to have left until 1878. Indians continued to plague settlers on the Texas frontier, and Hubbard administered a strong law enforcement program to stop them. He also approved the organization of the Texas Stockraisers' Association. In the Centennial Exposition of 1876 at Philadelphia, Hubbard was asked to deliver a speech, and he was instantly recognized as one of the best orators in America. When his term was over, Hubbard practiced law and continued his Democratic Party activities. He was appointed Minister to Japan by *President Cleveland* in 1885, where he served until 1889. He returned to Tyler and died there. He was the author of *The United States in the Far East*, 1899.

•HUDSPETH, CLAUDE BENTON, (1877-1941)- U. S. Representative, was born in Medina, Bandera County, Texas, May 12; attended the country schools; learned the printing trade; moved to Ozona, Texas, in 1893 and published the Ozona Kicker for a few years; employed as a cowboy; engaged in the cattle trading business and later in ranching, owning ranches in Brewster, Val Verde, Crockett, and Terrell Counties, Texas; member of the State house of representatives 1902-1906; served in the State senate 1906-1918 and was elected president of that body four times; studied law; was admitted to the bar in 1909 and commenced practice in El Paso, Texas; director of the Texan Oil & Land Co.; elected as a Democrat to the Sixty-sixth and to the five succeeding Congresses (March 4, 1919-March 3, 1931); was not a candidate for renomination in 1930; retired from active political and business pursuits in 1930 and resided in San Antonio, Texas, until his death there on March 19.

•HUTCHESON, JOSEPH CHAPPELL, (1842-1924)- U. S. Representative, was born near Boydton, Mecklenburg County, Va., May 18; attended the common schools; was graduated from Randolph-Macon College, Ashland, Va., in 1861; enlisted as a private in the Twenty-first Virginia Regiment during the Civil War; served in the Valley of Virginia under Stonewall Jackson and surrendered at Appomattox, at which time he was in command of Company E, Fourteenth Virginia Regiment; was graduated from the law department of the University of Virginia at Charlottesville in 1866; was admitted to the bar in 1866 and commenced practice in Anderson, Grimes County, Texas; moved to Houston, Texas, in 1874 and continued the practice of law; member of the State house of representatives in 1880; elected as a Democrat to the Fifty-third and Fifty-fourth Congresses (March 4, 1893-March 3, 1897); was not a candidate for renomination in 1896; resumed the practice of law in Houston, Texas; died at his summer home on Signal Mountain, near Chattanooga, Tenn., May 25.

I

•IKARD, FRANK NEVILLA, (1914-)- U. S. Representative, was born in Henrietta, Clay County, Texas, January 30; attended the public schools and Shriner Institute, Kerrville, Texas; University of Texas, A. B., 1936 and the law school, LL. B., 1936; was admitted to the bar in 1937 and commenced the practice of law in Wichita Falls, Texas; during World War II enlisted in the United States Army in January 1944 and served with Company K, One Hundred and Tenth Infantry, Twenty-eighth Division; prisoner of war in Germany in 1944 and 1945; awarded the Purple Heart Medal; was discharged from the service in December 1945; judge of Thirtieth Judicial District Court of Wichita Falls, Texas; chairman of Veterans Affairs Commission of Texas in 1948 and and 1949; Democratic presidential elector in 1948; appointed by Governor Beauford Jester in November 1948 judge of the Thirtieth District Court, subsequently elected in 1950, and served until September 8, 1951; delegate to the Democratic National Conventions in 1956, 1960, and 1968; chairman, Texas State Democratic Convention, 1960; elected as a Democrat to the Eighty-second Congress to fill the vacancy caused by the resignation of Ed Gossett; reelected to the Eighty-third and to the Four succeeding Congresses and served from September 8, 1951, to December 15, 1961, when he resigned; executive vice president of American Petroleum Institute, 1962-1963, president 1963 to present; member, board of regents, University of Texas System; is a resident of Wichita Falls, Texas.

•IRELAND, JOHN (1827-1896), seventeenth governor of Texas (1883-87), was born in Millerstown, Hart County, Kentucky to *Patrick and Rachel Newton Ireland,* farmers. He learned grammar at the local field school but spent most of his time working on the farm. When he was 18, he was declared of age to enable him to qualify as a policeman. This office he held for several years and also served as a deputy of Hart County in 1847-50. He then studied law with a firm in Mumfordsville, and in 1852 was admitted to the bar. Hoping to find more opportunity, he moved to Texas, settling in Seguin, where he soon gained respect as a lawyer and citizen. He married *Mrs. Matilda Wicks Faircloth* in 1854, and was elected Seguin's first mayor after incorporation. When Civil War broke out, he joined the Confederate side, having been a delegate to the secessionist constitutional convention of 1861. After the war, in which he was a lieutenant colonel, he was once again a constitutional framer in 1866, this time to regain admittance to the Union. That same year he was elected a district judge, but was removed as "an impediment to Reconstruction" in 1867. When the conservatives had regained power, Ireland was elected to the state legislature in 1873 and to the senate in 1874. He was appointed a justice of the Texas Supreme Court the next year, but declined reelection under the new constitution of 1876, which required the court consist of only three judges. In 1882 he was elected governor by a large majority, and immediately set about improving and building public institutions. He organized an office of the State Superintendant of Public Instruction, and placed school funds in investment bonds. He dealt with large cattlemen who fenced off public lands for their exclusive use, sent state troops to suppress a labor strike at Galveston in 1885 and a railroad strike at Fort Worth in 1887. Ireland decided not to run for a third term in office, but retired to Seguin with his second wife, *Anna Penn* and five children. Only two of these children survived him at the time of his death at San Antonio, Texas.

J

•JAWORSKI, LEON (1905-), lawyer and investigator, was born in Waco, Texas on September 19, 1905. He was educated at Baylor University and George Washington Univesity, receiving his law degree in 1926. During World War II he was a colonel in the Judge Advocate's Office, and served as Trial Judge Advocate in major war crimes trials held after the war. Returning to civilian life he joined a top Houston law firm and began an additional career as a special assistant to the U.S. Attorney General, and the Attorney General of Texas. Leon Jaworski achieved national fame as Director of the Watergate special prosecution force in 1973, which led up to the resignation of Richard Nixon. Mr. Jaworski is member of many boards of directors, as well as a member of the American Bar Association and past President of the Texas Bar Association. He is married and has three children.

•JESTER, BEAUFORT H. (1893-1949), thirty-fifth governor of Texas (1947-49), was born in Corsicana, Texas, the son of *George Taylor and Frances Gordon Jester*. He attended public schools in town and in 1916 finished his education at the University of Texas. He served as a captain with the U.S. Army for a while before attending law school (L.L.B., 1920). He opened a general practice in Corsicana in 1920, eventually representing large Texas oil companies in the region. By 1940 he was prominent enough to become the director of the state bar association, and he had served on the board of regents of the University of Texas since 1929. He was elected to the state Railroad Commission in 1942, remaining in that position until he became a candidate for governor in 1946. Once elected, Jester maintained the conservative attitude against new taxes. However, the economy was on his side, and he was able to approve more funding for state

101

hospitals and other public institutions with all of the excess money. Governor Jester also advocated some new regulations on labor unions and generally opposed New Deal programs and approaches. He also approved the founding of a Texas University for Negroes, and reorganized public education, with a new Youth Development Council for mobilizing and coordinating services for the young. Jester won easily in the 1948 election, but was unable to fill out his term; he died while traveling to Galveston in July 1949.

•JOHNSON, LYNDON B. (1908-73), thirty-sixth U.S. President, was known not only for his involvement of the U.S. in Vietnam, but also for the high aspirations of his "Great Society" programs. He was born on a hill country farm near Stonewall, Texas. Nearby also was the town his grandfather founded, Johnson City. His father, *Samuel*, was a state senator, and his mother *Rebekah*, was an elocution teacher. He was on the speech and debate team at his local high school, and after graduation took several odd jobs in Texas and California. In 1927, he began studies at Southwest Texas Teachers College in San Marcos, working his way through as a janitor and a secretary. For a year, he taught school in Cotulla, Texas, but in 1930 completed his studies with a B.S. degree in history. He taught public speaking and debate at a high school in Houston, and soon became interested in local Democratic politics. Representative *Richard Kleberg* brought him to Washington, D.C. in 1931 as his secretary. He began studying law at Georgetown University, and in 1935 was named a state administrator of the National Youth Administration by *President Roosevelt*. Johnson married *Claudia Alta Taylor*, nicknamed "Lady Bird" in 1934. In 1937, he ran for Congress as a New Deal Democrat, and took his seat in the shadow of a mentor, *Samuel Rayburn*. The young legislator supported measures for soil conservation, public housing, and aid to black farmers in Texas. Although he continued to hold his seat until 1946, Johnson also served on the Naval Reserve in Australia and New Zealand during World War II. On one mission, his plane was bombarded by Japanese bullets. After the war, he served on several military committees in the House, including the Joint Atomic Energy Committee in 1948. Later that same year, he was elected in an extremely close race for the U.S. Senate. Former Texas Governor *Coke Stevenson* contested Johnson's 87 vote majority in the Democratic primaries, but the election was certified. Johnson advanced rapidly in the senate and generally supported liberal reform measures, except when it came to the military. He was also a strong supporter of space research, and was named chair of the Aeronautical and Space Sciences Committee in 1959-60. Soon after becoming Senate majority leader in 1955, Johnson suffered a heart attack, but recovered quickly enough to return to his post within a few months. He was known as a master of the legislative process and of tactical compromise, especially while Republican *President Eisenhower* was in office. His major action of the late 1950s was in securing the passage of the Civil Rights Acts of 1957 and 1960. In the latter year, he tried for the Democratic presidential nomination, and after he lost, he surprised many of his colleagues by becoming *John Kennedy's* running mate. His influence in the Southern U.S. helped *Kennedy* win over Republican candidate *Richard Nixon*. As with most vice presidents, Johnson kept a low profile in 1961-63, although he was active with NASA and the President's Committee on Equal Employment Opportunity. He took part in the policy decisions during the Cuban missile crisis as well. Still, he was not prepared for November 22, 1963, when *John Kennedy* was assassinated in Dallas, and within a half hour he was sworn in as President. The next few months were spent in trying to gain passage of several of the late President's measures. Soon after, President Johnson embarked on his own series of plans and programs which he hoped would bring about a "Great Society" in America. More antipoverty measures, civil rights laws, and fair employment legislation were passed in the next decade than ever before. However, a dark cloud hung over the Johnson administration after 1964, when he ordered retaliatory military action against the North Vietnamese army, which had reportedly attacked U.S. Navy ships in the South China Sea. Under the "Gulf of Tonkin Resolution," Johnson was then empowered to use force whenever he deemed necessary in the region. This act later became the catalyst which brought on a full-scale war in Vietnam, as Johnson ordered more and more U.S. troops into the area. Although Johnson won by a large majority in his 1964 election, by 1968 he had lost much of his popularity. The early primaries resulted so poorly for him that he announced that he would not run for reelection. However, his Vice President, *Hubert Humphrey*, won the Democratic nomination that year. Johnson returned to his ranch in the Hill Country of Texas. He spent the remainder of his time tending his herd of Herefords as well as his other financial holdings, and continued his activities in the Democratic party. He wrote his memoirs in the book, *Vantage Point* in 1971. Many of his speeches are collected in the 1964 book, *My Hope For America*.

•JOHNSTON, RIENZI MELVILLE, (1849-1926)- (cousin of Benjamin Edward Russell)- U. S. Senator, was born in Sandersville, Washington County, Ga., September 9; attended the public schools; during the Civil WEar served in the Confederate Army; moved to Austin, Texas, in 1878 and engaged in journalism; moved to Houston in 1883 and established the Houston Post; member of the Democratic National Committee 1900-1912; appointed as a Democrat to the United States Senate to fill the vacancy caused by the resignation of Joseph W. Bailey and served from January 4 to February 2, 1913, when a successor was elected and qualified; resumed his former activities as editor and president of the Houston Post; relinquished the active management of his newspaper business in 1919 and lives in retirement until his death in Houston, Texas, February 28.

•JONES, GEORGE WASHINGTON, (1828-1903)- U. S. Representative, was born in Marion County, Ala., September 5; moved with his parents to Tipton County, Tenn., and shortly afterward to Bastrop, Texas, in 1848; attended the common schools; studied law; was admitted to the bar in 1851 and commenced practice in Bastrop, Texas; elected district attorney in 1856; during the Civil War enlisted in the Confederate Army as a private; commissioned lieutenant colonel and afterward promoted to the colonelcy of the Seventeenth Texas Infantry; returned to Bastrop County; member of the State constitutional convention in 1866; elected Lieutenant Governor of Texas in 1866; removed by General Sheridan as "an impediment to reconstruction" in 1867; elected on the Greenback Party ticket to the Forty-sixth and Forty-seventh Congresses (March 4, 1879-March 3, 1883); was not a candidate for reelection in 1882 to the Forty-eighth Congress; resumed the practice of his profession in Bastrop, Texas, and died there July 11.

•JONES, JAMES HENRY, (1830-1904)- U. S. Representative, was born in Shelby County, Ala., September 13; moved with his parents to Talladega County, Ala., in early youth; pursued an academic course; studied law; was admitted to the bar in 1851 and commenced practice in Henderson, Texas; during the civil War enlisted in the Confederate Army and served as captain, lieutenant colonel, and colonel of the eleventh Texas Infantry; presidential elector on the Democratic ticket of Hancock and English in 1880; elected as a Democrat to the Forty-eighth and Forty-ninth Congresses (March 4, 1883-March 3, 1887); resumed the practice of law in Henderson, Texas, and died there March 22.

•JONES, JOHN MARVIN, (1886-)- U. S. Representative, was born near Valley View, Cooke County, Texas, February 26; attended the common schools; John B. Denton College, A. B., 1902; Southwestern University, Georgetown, Texas, B.S., 1905; the law department of the University of Texas at Austin, LL. B., 1907; was admitted to the bar the same year and commenced practice in Amarillo, Texas; appointed a member of the board of legal examiners for the seventh supreme judicial district of Texas in 1913; member of the Democratic National Congressional Campaign Committee; served during the First World War as a private in Company A, Three Hundred and Eighth Battalion of the Tank Corps, in 1918; elected as a Democrat to the Sixty-fifth and the the eleven succeeding Congresses and served from March 4, 1917, until his resignation on November 20, 1940, to become a judge of the United States Court of Claims, having been appointed to that office by President Franklin D. Roosevelt; on leave from the Court of Claims beginning January 15, 1943, served as adviser and assistant to the Director of Economic Stabilization until June 29, 1943, when he was appointed administrator of the United States War Food Administration and served until July 1, 1945, when he resumed his duties as judge of the United States Court of Claims, serving as chief judge from July 10, 1947, until his retirement July 14, 1964; special master, United States Supreme Court for Mississippi and Louisiana, 1965; is a legal resident of Amarillo, Texas.

•**JOPLIN, JANIS** (1943-79), singer of the blues, was known for her high powered scratchy wail, which she used on such songs as "Love is Like a Ball and Chain", "Piece of My Heart", and the inimitable "Bobby McGee". Born to a middle-class family in the oil refining town of Port Arthur, Texas, she grew bored with her surroundings as a teenager, and ran away to Houston, although she returned home within a month. The business courses she had begun in her hometown enabled her to move to Los Angeles with confidence about supporting herself. This she did, between periods in the unemployment lines, as a keypunch operator. It wasn't until she recieved encouragement at a party (after imitating blues singer Odetta) that she thought of singing for a living. But her money was low in 1965, forcing her to return to Port Arthur. Joplin took a few courses at Lamar State College in Beaumont, but soon left again for California after joining a band called Big Brother with an old friend, *Travis Rivers.* Her wild singing style was a hit with the "hippies" of Haight-Ashbury in San Francisco. Some reviewers heard "some deep dark region of her Texas soul" in her music. Big Brother became well known in the rock club circuit of the nation after its appearance at the Monterey Pop Festival of 1967. Their first Columbia album was released in 1968, called *Cheap Thrills* ; it was a sellout from the beginning. Joplin left the band in late 1968, however, and went on to perform with another group in the next two years. A heavy drinker and drug user, she once predicted, "Maybe I won't last as long as other singers, but I think you can destroy your now by worrying about tomorrow." She died of a drug overdose in October, 1970.

•**JORDAN, BARBARA** (1934 -), U.S. Representative, (1973 -) was born in Houston, Texas to the *Reverend Benjamin and Arlyne Patten Jordan.* As she grew up, she became more and more aware of the second class status of her race in Texas, although she was able to compete as an equal in the all-black schools she attended. At Phillis Wheatley High School, Ms. Jordan was active on the speech and debate team, and was president of the school's national Honor Society chapter. She received a B.A. degree in Government from Texas A & I University, but decided that if she wanted to become successful, she would have to go to an Eastern school to study law. After three difficult years of study, she received her L.L.B. from Boston University in 1959. She established a small practice at home in Houston after passing both the Massachussetts and Texas bar exams, and taught classes in government at the Tuskegee Institute. In 1962 and 1964, she ran unsuccessfully for the state legislature, but remained active in the Democratic party. A fellow politician informed her that she had too much against her because she was black, a woman, and large. She replied that she couldn't do anything about two of those things, and proceeded to campaign for state senate, this time successfully, in 1966. Her district was comprised of a working class minority neighborhood of Houston. Her work in Austin brought her in conflict with *John Connally's* politics, and in sync with those of *President Johnson.* In fact, Johnson invited her to a special meeting at the White House on fair housing legislation as early as 1967. *Johnson* later supported her race for a U.S. congressional seat in 1972. In office, she continued to support fair housing laws, voting rights, bilingual education, fair trade, and general civil rights laws. Perhaps Jordan's most important work in Congress was her involvement with the Watergate Judiciary Committee Hearings on the impeachment of *President Richard Nixon.* On June 25, 1974, she presented her position on impeachment to the press, saying, "Today I am an inquisitor... My faith in the Constitution is whole. It is total. I am not going to sit here and be a idle spectator to the dimunition, the subversion, the destruction of the Constitution... Has the President committed offenses and planned and directed and acquiesced in a course of conduct which the Constitution will not tolerate? That is the question... We know the question. We should now forthwith proceed to answer the question." Representative Jordan was again in the public spotlight--this time on a much happier note--at the 1976 Democratic National convention as the keynote speaker. When *Jimmy Carter* was elected President, he asked her what she would like to do in his administration, and she replied that she would not take anything less than Attorney General. Rumors in the press about Jordan's affiliation with Texas oil interests and poor relationship with the Congressional Black Caucus probably ruined her chances for that post, but she continued on in her seat, serving on various committees until 1978. She has been awarded numerous honorary PhD degrees from such institutions as Princeton and Harvard, and was *Time* magazine's Woman of the Year in 1975. Since 1979, she has been a Public Service professor at the Lyndon B. Johnson School of Public Affairs in Austin, Texas. She also hosts the Public Television documentary series, "Crisis to Crisis."

K

•**KAUFMAN, DAVID SPANGLER,** (1813-1851)- U. S. Representative, was born in Boiling Springs, Cumberland County, Pa., December 18; pursued classical studies, and was graduated from Princeton College in 1833; studied law; was admitted to the bar in Natchez, Miss., and commenced practice in Natchitoches, La.; moved to Nacogdoches, Republic of Texas, in 1837; served against the Indians; member of the Texas House of Representatives 1839-1843; served in the Texas Senate 1843-1845; appointed Charge d' Affaires of Texas to the United States in 1845; moved to Lowes Ferry, Texas; upon the admission of Texas as a State into the Union was elected as a Democrat to the Twenty-ninth Congress; reelected to the Thirtieth and Thirty-first Congresses and served from March 30, 1846, until his death in Washington, D. C., on January 31.

•**KAZEN, ABRAHAM, JR.,** (1919-)- U. S. Representative, Democrat, of Laredo, Texas; was born in Laredo, January 17; graduate of Laredo High School, 1937; attended the University of Texas, 1937-40; Cumberland University Law School in Lebanon, Tenn., 1941; member of the State Bar of Texas since 1942; member of law firm, Raymond, Alvarado & Kazen, 1946-55; practiced in own law office since that time; son of Lebanese parents, speaks Spanish and Arabic; commissioned an Air Force pilot; during World War II served in North Africa, Sicily, and Italy as a pilot in Troop Carrier Command; later served as the personal pilot for Gen. Sir Oliver Leese, commander of the British 8th Army in Italy, and in India and Burma when General Leese commanded Allied ground forces in the China-Burma-India theater; flew a total of 1,700 hours overseas; and finished his duty by serving as an instrument instructor pilot at Love Field in Dallas;

discharged with the rank of captain; served in the Texas House of Representatives 1947-52; elected to the senate of Texas, 1952, and served continuously for 14 years through 1966; served as chairman or vice chairman of every important committee; elected president pro tempore of senate, 1959; served as Acting Governor of Texas, August 4, 1959; member of Texas Legislative Council for 16 years; sponsor of preschool program for non-English-speaking children; named Man of the Year and also Father of the Year in his hometown of Laredo; married Consuelo Raymond of Laredo; five children: Abraham II, Mrs. E. C. Dillman, Jr., Mrs. Ronald Attal, Catherine, and Jo-Betsy; member of Laredo and Texas Bar Associations, American Legion, V.F.W., Knights of Columbus, University of Texas Ex-Students Association; elected to the 90th Congress November 8, 1966; reelected to 91st, 92d, and 93d Congresses.

•**KENDALL, GEORGE W.** (1809-1867), journalist during the Mexican War, was born in New Hampshire. He worked as a printer's apprentice in Vermont, Washington D.C., and New York before moving south in 1843 to Alabama to escape a yellow fever epidemic in New York City. He later moved to New Orleans, Louisiana for four years, helped found a newspaper, and joined the Santa Fe trading expedition in 1841. After a struggle, the Santa Fe crew was captured by Mexicans and held prisoner for two years. Kendall wrote a *Narrative of the Texan Santa Fe Expedition* soon after his release.

In 1846 the Mexican War broke out and Kendall began developing the first modern system of war correspondence. On muleback from Algiers, Louisiana, he set out for the Rio Grande to join *General Zachary Taylor.* On the way, he organized a chain of pony express riders by whom - and also by ships - he sent back news stories which so "scooped" the other American papers that the latest war news in even the largest New York journals was frequently preceded by: "The *New Orleans Picayune* says." He participated in battles, personally captured a Mexican cavalry flag, was wounded in the fighting which preceded the capture of Mexico City, and entered the city with *General Winfield Scott.* The climax of his successful exploits was that news of the American victory reached Washington by pony express from the *Picayune* ahead of official despatches, and the Treaty of Guadalupe was published in that paper before the U.S. Government had received its text. Following the war he went to France, whence he sent letters on European affairs. On his return, although he retained his financial interest in the *Picayune* and made further short visits to Europe, he made his home for the remainder of his life at Berne. Much of present Kendall County was his ranch.

•KILDAY, PAUL JOSEPH, (1900-1968)- U. S. Representative, was born in Sabinal, Uvalde County, Texas, March 29; moved with his parents to San Antonio, Texas, in 1904; attended the public and parochial schools and St. Mary's College, San Antonio, Texas; employed as a clerk, United States Air Force, Washington, D.C., 1918-1921 and as a law clerk, United States Shipping Board Emergency Fleet Corporation, in 1921 and 1922; was graduated from the law department of Georgetown University, Washington, D. C., in 1922; was admitted to the bar the same year and commenced practice in San Antonio, Texas; served as first assistant district attorney of Bexar County, Texas, 1935-1938; elected as a Democrat to the Seventy-sixth and to the eleven succeeding Congresses and served from January 3, 1939, until his resignation September 24, 1961, having been appointed a judge of the Court of Military Appeals and served in this capacity until his death in Washington, D. C., October 12.

•KLEBERG, RUDOLPH, (1847-1924)- (great uncle of Robert Christian Eckhardt, uncle of Richard Mifflin Kleberg, Sr.)- U. S. Representative, was born in Cat Spring, Austin County, Texas, on June 26; instructed by private tutors; was graduated from Concrete College De Witt County, in 1868; enlisted in Tom Green's brigade of Cavalry in the Confederate Army in the spring of 1864 and served until the close of the Civil War; studied law in San Antonio, Texas; was admitted to the bar in 1872 and commenced practice in Cuero, Texas; established the Cuero Star in 1873; prosecuting attorney of De Witt County 1876-1890; member of the State senate 1882-1886; appointed United States attorney for the

western district of Texas in 1885; elected as a Democrat to the
Fifty-fourth Congress to fill the vacancy caused by the death of
William II. Crain; reelected to the Fifty-fifth, Fifty-sixth, and
Fifty-seventh Congresses and served from April 7, 1896, to March
3, 1903; was not a candidate for renomination in 1902; resumed
the practice of law; moved to Austin, Texas, in 1905; appointed
official reporter for the court of criminal appeals February 24,
1905, and served until his death in Austin, December 28.

•KRUEGER, ROBERT CHALRES, (1935-)- U. S. Representa-
tive, Democrat, of New Braunfels, Texas, born in New
Braunfels, September 19; graduated New Braunfels High School,
1953; B.A., Southern Methodist University, 1957; M.A., Duke
University, 1958; B. Litt., 1961, Ph.D., Oxford University,
England, 1964; until 1973, associate professor of English and vice
provost and dean of the College of Arts and Sciences, Duke
University; currently, board chairman of Comal Hosiery Mills;
partner, Krueger Brangus Ranch; author-editor, "The Poems of
Sir John Davies"; member: New Braunfels Lions Club, Optimist
Club, West Texas Chamber of Commerce, San Antonio Chamber
of Commerce, American Marketing Association, American
Association of Higher Education, Modern Language Association,
and Modern Humanities Research Association; elected to the
94th Congress, November 5, 1974.

L

•LAGRONE, CYRUS WILSON, JR. (1911-), educator, was born at Paint Rock, Texas on January 8, 1911. He was educated at the University of Texas, taking his Ph.D there in 1932. Following his doctorate he taught at the University of Texas. During World War II he served in the Army as a lieutenant colonel. Upon reentry to civilian life, Dr. Lagrone taught at the University of Southern California and Texas Christian Univesity. He is amember of the American Psychology Association, Southwestern Psychology Association, and the Texas Board of Psychology Examiners. He has contributed numerous articles to professional journals in his specialty. He is married and makes his home in Fort Worth.

•LAMAR, MIRABEAU BOUNAPARTE (1798-1859), second President of the Republic of Texas (1838-41), was born in Louisville, Georgia, the son of Huguenot parents who were fond of naming their children after historical figures. He spent his boyhood on a farm and had little of the formal education he later advocated for Texas. His first important job was a publisher of a states-rights journal, the *Columbus Independent*, known for its radical opinions against a Central American government. He grew interested in the growing crisis Texas, and resettled there. Before long, he was involved in the revolutionary movement. In the battle of San Jacinto, April 21, 1836, he led the charge of cavalry that broke the Mexican ranks. *General Houston* recognized his abilities, and he was promoted to major general. He was attorney-general and then secretary of war of Texas under *President Burnet*, and on *Houston's* accession to the presidency became vice president, as *Houston* declared, on the strength of his bravery in the Battle of San Jacinto. In 1838, he was elected president to succeed *Houston*, and began an administration noted principally for extravagant schemes and disastrous consequences. Unlike *Houston*, Lamar believed that the Indians should be severely dealt with, and he ordered such drastic measures against them that they began to hate all of the white settlers. When Lamar heard that the Mexican government was aiding the Cherokees against the Texans, he directed a series of massacres that eventually drove the Indians out of Texas. The Comanches were also troublesome to Lamar. Their chiefs were invited to send a committee to San Antonio for negotiation. Although they were supposed to bring all of their white prisoners with them, they brought only one white girl, who testified that there were many other whites held by the tribe. This led to a fight, and finally the chiefs denying the charge were arrested and shot to death. When other Indians protested the executions, they were also killed by Lamar's troops. A series of raids by the Comanches followed, until August, 1839, when they were completely routed by troops under *General Houston* and *Colonel Burleson*, at the Battle of Plum Creek. Still not satisfied with this victory for the Texans, Lamar insisted on sending an expedition to New Mexico in order to overthrow the Mexican government there so they could join with Texas. This action was opposed by the congress and *Sam Houston* and met defeat at the hands of Mexican *General Salezar*. To carry on these and other expensive enterprises, the annual expenses rose as high as $900,000 on an income of $180,000 and at the close of Lamar's administration the public debt was far into the millions. On the other hand, during this period the commercial prospects of the republic grew steadily brighter, and the export trade increased. In 1839, he made the first move to establish a public school system, and in 1840 the state university was founded. The capital was moved from Houston to Austin. Lamar was bitterly opposed to annexation to the U.S.; calling it "the grave of all Texas' hopes of happiness and greatness." He grew ill toward the end of his administration, but he recuperated enough by 1846 to participate in the Battle of Monterrey. After 1847 he was stationed in command of an independent company of Texas Rangers at Laredo. In 1855-56, he was U.S. Minister to Argentina, but returned to his plantation in Fort Bend County. The remainder of his life was devoted to his literary interests. His volume of *Verse Memorials* (1857) contains several romantic poems, notably "The Daughter of Mendoza." Lamar's personal letters were included with his Presidential papers in *The Papers of Mirabeau Buonaparte Lamar*, published in 1922 through 1927.

•LANHAM, FRITZ GARLAND, (1880-1965)- (son of Samuel Willis Tucker Lanham)- U. S. Representative, was born in Weatherford, Texas, January 3; attended the public schools of Washington, D.C., and was graduated from Weatherford College, Weatherford, Texas, in 1897; attended Vanderbilt University in 1897 and 1898, and was graduated from the University of Texas at Austin in 1900, subsequently taking a law course in the same institution; was admitted to the bar in 1909 and commenced practice in Weatherford, Texas; moved to Fort Worth, Texas, in 1917; elected as a Democrat to the sixty-sixth Congress to fill the vacancy caused by the resignation of James C. Wilson; reelected to the Sixty-seventh and to the twelve succeeding Congresses and served from April 19, 1919, to January 3, 1947; was not a candidate for renomination in 1946; engaged as an adviser on legislation in Washington, D. C., until 1961; moved to Austin, Texas, where he died July 31.

•LANHAM, SAMUEL W.T. (1846-1908), twenty-second governor of Texas, (1903-07), was born in Spartanburg, South Carolina to *James M. and Louisa Tucker Lanham.* He studied at public schools until the Civil War interrupted his education and he signed with the Third South Carolina regiment. After the war, he moved to Texas and married *Sarah Meng* and began to study law when he wasn't teaching school. Lanham was admitted to the Texas bar in 1869 and opened an office in Red River County. In 1883, he was elected to the U.S. House of Representatives, and served until 1893 and again in 1897-1903. He left Washington to become governor of Texas, the last Civil War veteran to take that seat. The governor was concerned with the state election codes of the time, and he helped lay the foundation for Texas' present election laws during his administration, providing for primary elections and filing of candidates' campaign expenditures among other measures. A major oil field was unplugged while Lanham was governor, and so he witnessed the birth of Texas' future economy. After his second term, Lanham retired with his wife and five children to Weathertop, Texas, where he died.

•LEATH, JAMES MARVIN, (1931-)- U. S. Representative, Democrat, of Marlin, Texas; was born in Henderson, May 6; attended the public schools; graduated Henderson High School, Henderson, Texas, 1949; attended Kilgore Junior College; B.B.A., University of Texas, Austin, Texas, 1954; attended college on football scholarship, member of 1953 Southwest Conference and Cotton Bowl championship team at University of Texas; freshman line coach at University of Texas, 1953-54; commissioner officer, U.S. Army, 1954-56; coached football and track, Henderson High School, 1957-59; entered business as salesman, 1959; banking, 1962, officer and director in five Texas banks, and two manufacturing companies; served 2 years as special assistant to U.S. Congressman W. R. Poage, 1972-74; very active in community and industrial development throughout central Texas; elder in Presbyterian Church; married to the former Alta Ruth Neill, 1954; one son, Thomas, oldest son, Jim, born 1960, died of leukemia in 1970; elected to the 96th Congress, November 7, 1978; reelected to the 97th and 98th Congresses.

•LEE, HECTOR (1908-), educator, was born in Decatur, Texas on May 16, 1908. He was educated at the University of Utah and New Mexico, where he received his Ph.D in 1947. He taught at Chico State University, and Sonoma State as a Professor of English. His specialty is forklore, and his is Vice Presient of the California Folklore Society. He is the author of several books and many articles on folklore. He is married and has one son.

•LEE, ROBERT QUINCY, (1869-1930)- U. S. Representative, was born near Coldwater, Tate County, Miss., January 12; attended the public schools and the Fort Worth (Texas) High School; moved with his father to Fort Worth, Texas, in 1886, and to Caddo, Stephens County, Texas, in 1891; engaged in the general merchandise business; moved to Cisco, Eastland County, Texas, in 1913 and engaged in ranching, agricultural pursuits, and banking; founder and builder in 1919 of the Cisco & Northeastern Railroad Co., and served as its president 1919-1927; president of the West Texas Chamber of Commerce in 1926 and 1927; elected as a Democrat to the Seventy-first Congress and served from March 4, 1929, until his death in Washington, D. C., April 18.

•LELAN, GEORGE THOMAS (MICKEY), (1944-)- U. S. Representative, Democrat, of Houston, Texas; was born in Lubbock, November 27; attended the public schools; graduated, Phillis Wheatley Senior High School, Houston, Texas, 1963; B.S., pharmacy, Texas Southern University, Houston, Texas, 1970; senior vice president, King State Bank; director, Hermann Hospital; State representative, Texas District 88, 1972-79; delegate, Democratic National Conventions in Miami (1976), New York (1980); 63d-65th legislative sessions-labor committee, human resources committee; member, legislative council board; vice chairman, joint committee on prison reform; 1974 Texas Constitutional Convention; member, rights and sufferages committee; member, interim legislative council study committee; interim committee on occupational health and safety and law enforcement education and standards; served on house appropriations committee; committee on health and welfare; legislative budget board; elected to 1976 Democratic National Committee (DNC), reelected 1980; currently serves as chairman, DNC Black Caucus; chairman, DNC Commission on Low and Moderate Income Participation (Leland Commission), cofounder, cochair, DNC Black-Hispanic Caucus; elected, first vice-chairman, Congressional Black Caucus (CBC), 1983; chairman, CBC Energy Braintrust; Honorary Doctor of Humane Letters, Texas Southern University, Houston, Texas, 1982; member: Menil Foundation; Hope Development, Inc.; Black Arts Center; Energy Conservation Society; Community Advisory Committee; E. O. Smith Junior High; Educational Advancement for Mexican Americans; Houston Council on Human Relations; Policy Advisory Committee; Senior Citizens Inc.; Texas Association of Developing Colleges, UNCF; Greater Northside Task Force; Black Communicators Association; elected to the 96th Congress, November 7, 1978; reelected to the 97th and 98th Congresses; elected freshman majority whip, 96th Congress; elected majority whip at-large, 97th Congress.

•LIVELY, ROBERT MACLIN, (1855-1929)- U. S. Representative, was born in Fayetteville, Washington County, Ark., on January 6; moved to Texas in 1864 with his parents, who settled in Smith County; attended private schools in eastern Texas; studied law; was admitted to the bar in 1876 and commenced practice in Kaufman, Kaufman County, Texas; moved to Canton, Van Zandt County, and continued the practice of law; prosecuting attorney of Van Zandt County 1882-1884; elected as a Democrat to the Sixty-first Congress to fill the vacancy caused by the resignation of J. Gordon Russell and served from July 23, 1910, to March 3, 1911; declined to be a candidate for renomination in 1910; judge of Van Zandt County, Texas, 1916-1918; died in Canton, Texas, January 15.

•LOEFFLER, TOM, (1945-)- U. S. Representative, Republican, of Hunt, Texas; born in Fredericksburg August 1; son of Gilbert and Marie Loeffler; attended the public schools in Mason, Texas; B.B.A., University of Texas, Austin, Texas, 1968; J.D., University of Texas Law School, 1971; lawyer and rancher; Legal Counsel, U.S. Department of Commerce, 1971-72; chief legislative counsel to U.S. Senator John Tower of Texas, 1972-74; Deputy for Congressional Affairs, Federal Energy Administration, 1974-75; Special Assistant for Legislative Affairs to President Gerald Ford, 1975-77; Washington counsel, Tenneco, Inc., 1977; partner, Banister & Loeffler, 1977-78; admitted to the State Bar of Texas in 1971; member: Texas and American Bar Associations; member, bar of the District of Columbia Court of Appeals; Lutheran; married to the former Kathy Crawford of McAllen, Texas; two sons, Lance and Cullen; chief deputy Republican whip; elected to the 96th Congress, November 7, 1978; reelected to the 97th and 98th Congresses.

•LONG, JOHN BENJAMIN, (1843-1924)- U. S. Representative, was born in Douglass, Nacogdoches County, Texas, September 8; moved with his parents to Rusk, Texas, in 1846; educated in private schools; during the Civil War served in the Confederate Army in Company C, Third Texas Cavalry; was twice severely wounded; studied law; was admitted to the bar but never practiced; became a planter; elected as a Democrat to the Fifty-second Congress (March 4, 1891-March 3, 1893); unsuccessful candidate for renomination in 1892; engaged in the newspaper business in Rusk, Texas, 1886-1905; member of the State house of representatives in 1913 and 1914; died in Rusk, Cherokee County, Texas, April 27.

•LUBBOCK, FRANCIS R. (1815-1905), eighth governor of Texas (1861-63), was a native of Beaufort, South Carolina. His parents were *Henry T.W. and Susan Ann Saltus Lubbock,* planters. He attended public schools until the age of 14, when his father died and he was forced to look for a means to support the family. He was hired at a hardware store in Charleston at a salary of $12.50 per month. three years later he moved to Hamburg to join in another mercantile business, where he was in charge of a cotton warehouse. In 1834, he moved again to New Orleans and became a partner in a drugstore enterprise. The next year he married *Adele Baron* and eventually became involved in the jewelry business as well. Lubbock's brother had gone to Texas to aid in the Mexican War, but disappeared, and so Francis went after him to find out what had happened. He liked Texas so much that he remained and opened two drugstores in Velasco and Houston. He also bought a ranch in the region and soon became involved in the fighting against Mexico and the Indians. He was elected clerk to the Texas House of Representatives and in 1837 was made chief of the clerks. *President Houston* appointed Lubbock comptroller of the Treasury of the new republic soon afterwards. In mid 1841 Harris County elected him district clerk, a position he held for 17 years. In 1857, Lubbock was elected Lieutenant Governor, and when his term was up he retired to his ranch for a while before becoming active in the secessionist movement. In 1861 he was elected governor; he served only one term since he had decided that he could do more for the Confederacy by fighting with the Army. He entered service as assistant adjutant general under *General J.B. Magruder* and then under *General John Wharton*, fighting in Louisiana and later Virginia. At Richmond, Lubbock and *Jefferson Davis* were captured by the Union Army, and were held for eight months at Fort Delaware. He was able to return home to Houston by Christmas 1865. After the War, Lubbock retired to a private life of ranching and new industrial activities. He ran a large cotton compress company, and built a beef packing plant in Anahuac, which he managed for two years. In 1874, he was made president of the New York and Texas Beef Preserving Company, and was sent to Europe to gain new contracts. In 1878, Lubbock returned to public life as state treasurer of the Democratic ticket, serving until 1891. He had remarried *Sarah Black Porter* in 1883 after his first wife died. Although he held no more elective offices, Lubbock served as an advisor on the board of pardon and as one of the managers of the local Confederate veterans' home. He spent his last years in Austin; when his second wife died, he married once more, in 1903 to *Lue Scott*. She survived him after his death at home.

•LUCAS, WINGAGTE HEZEKIAH, (1908-)- U. S. Representative, was born in Grapevine, Tarrant County, Texas, May 1; attended the public schools, the North Texas Teachers College at Denton, the Oklahoma Agricultural and Mechanical College at Stillwater, and the Texas University at Austin; studied law; was admitted to the bar in 1938 and commenced practice in Grapevine, Texas; during World War II served as an enlisted man in the United States Army from 1943 to 1945 with overseas service in the European theater of operations; resumed the practice of law; elected as a Democrat to the Eightieth and to the three succeeding Congresses (January 3, 1947-January 3, 1955); unsuccessful candidate for renomination in 1954; resumed the practice of law; in 1958 moved to New York as corporate executive; in 1966 became executive director of the Mid-Appalachia College Council; is a resident of Bristol, Tenn.

•LYLE, JOHN EMMETT, JR., (1910-)- U. S. Representative, was born in Boyd, Wise County, Texas, September 1; attended the public schools, Wichita Falls High School, the Junior College at Wichita Falls, the University of Texas at Austin, and the Houston (Texas) Law School; was admitted to the bar in 1934 and commenced practice in Corpus Christi, Texas; served in the State house of representatives from January 1941 until his resignation in 1942, when he enlisted in the United States Army; served as an operations officer in the Five Hundred and Thirty-sixth Antiaircraft Battalion in the European theater until October 1944; elected as a Democrat to the Seventy-ninth and to the four succeeding Congresses (January 3, 1945-January 3, 1955); was not a candidate for renomination in 1954 to the Eighty-fourth Congress; resumed the practice of law; is a resident of Corpus Christi, Texas.

M

•MAHON, GEORGE H., (1900-)- U. S. Representative, Democrat, Lubbock, Texas; was born September 22 near Haynesville, La., son of J. K. and Lola Brown Mahon; moved to Mitchell County, Texas, 1908; reared on a farm; attended rural school, graduated from Loraine High School; B.A., Simmons University, Abilene, 1924; LL.B., University of Texas, 1925; attended University of Minnesota in 1925; honorary LL.D. 1951 Waynesburg College, Pennsylvania; honorary LL.D. 1960 Wayland Baptist College, Plainview, Texas; honorary LL.D. 1962 Texas Technological College, Lubbock, Texas; honorary LL.D. 1964 Hardin-Simmons University, Abilene, Texas; honorary LL.D. 1965 Pepperdine College, Los Angeles, Calif.; married Helen Stevenson, of Loraine, Texas, 1923; one daughter -Daphne, born 1927; elected county attorney, Mitchell County, 1926; appointed district Attorney, thirty-second judicial district, 1927; elected district attorney 1928, 1930, 1932; received American Political Science Association Congressional Distinguished Service Award in 1963; received the George Washington award of the American Good Government Society in 1969; in 1973, presented with the Congressional Distinguished Public Service Award of the American Legion; elected in 1934 to 74th Congress and reelected to each succeeding Congress; became chairman of Appropriations Committee of the House of Representatives in 1964, continuing in that capacity through the 93d Congress; chairman of the Joint Senate-House Committee on Reduction of Federal Expenditures; Regent of the Smithsonian Institution; in 1968 served on the President's Commission on Budget Concepts.

124

•MANN, THOMAS CLIFTON (1912-), ambassador, was born on November 11, 1912 in Laredo, Texas. He was educated at Baylor University, and received a law degree in 1934. After a short stint in legal practice he joined the State Department as a special assistant to the ambassdor to Uruguay. He returned to the U.S. in 1943 to take up duties as a State Department service officer. Mr. Mann was ambassador to El Salvador in 1955-57, and ambassdor to Mexico in 1961-63. He was a senior visiting scholar to the John Hopkins School of Advanced International Studies in 1966-67. Retiring from the government's service he became President of the Automobile Manufacturer's Association in 1967. Mr. Mann is married and has one son.

•MANSFIELD, JOSEPH JEFFERSON, (1861-1947)- U. S. Representative, was born in Wayne, Wayne County, Va. (now West Virginia), February 9; attended the public schools; moved to Alleyton, Texas, in 1881; employed as a farm and nursery laborer and later as a baggage-master and freight clerk with the Southern Pacific Railway; studied law; was admitted to the bar in 1886 and commenced practice at Eagle Lake, Texas; also established the first newspaper in that city; organized two companies of the National Guard of Texas in 1886; received commissions successively as second lieutenant, first lieutenant, and captain, and was appointed adjutant of the Fourth Texas Regiment with the rank of captain; prosecuting attorney of Colorado County 1892-1896; ex officio county superintendent of schools 1896-1910; judge of Colorado County 1896-1916; elected as a Democrat to the Sixty-fifth and to the fifteen succeeding Congresses and served from March 4, 1917, until his death in the naval hospital at Bethesda, Md., July 12.

•MATTOX, JAMES ALBON (JIM), (1943-)- U. S. Representative, Democrat, of Dallas, Texas; was born in Dallas, August 29; educated in the public schools of Dallas, Texas; graduated, Woodrow Wilson High School, 1961; graduated magna cum laude, Baylor University, Waco, Texas, 1965; J. D., Southern Methodist

University School of Law, Dallas, Texas, 1968; admitted to the bar in 1968 and began private practice in 1970; partner in law firm of Crowder, Mattox & Morris; lifelong member of the East Grand Baptist Church, Dallas, Texas, lay preacher; member Christian Life Commission; congressional intern in the office of the Honorable Earle Cabell, U. S. Representative from Texas, 1967; assistant district attorney, Dallas, Texas, 1968-70; elected State representative, 1972; reelected, 1974; elected to the 95th Congress, November 2, 1976; reelected to the 96th Congress; member: Budget and Banking, Finance and Urban Affairs Committees.

•MAVERICK, FONTAINE MAURY, (1895-1954)- (cousin of Abram P. Maury, nephew of James L. Slayden, and cousin of John W. Fishburne)- U. S. Representative, was born in San Antonio, Texas, October 23; attended the common schools of Texas, Virginia Military Institute at Lexington, and the University of Texas at Austin; studied law; was admitted to the bar in 1916 and commenced practice in San Antonio, Texas; during the First World War served as a first lieutenant in the One Hundred and Fifty-seventh Infantry, Fortieth Division, and was overseas with the Twenty-eighth Infantry, First Division; was wounded in action and discharged on February 7, 1919; was awarded the Silver Star and the Purple Heart Medal; engaged in the lumber, building-material, housing, and mortgage businesses 1925-1930; collector of taxes of Bexar County, Texas, 1929-1931; delegate to several Democratic State conventions and to the Democratic National Conventions in 1928 and 1940; elected as a Democrat to the Seventy-fourth and Seventy-fifth Congresses (January 3, 1935-January 3, 1939); unsuccessful candidate for renomination in 1938; mayor of San Antonio 1939-1941; divisional director and later vice chairman of the War Production Board and chairman of the Smaller War Plants Corporation, Washington, D. C., 1941-1946; resumed the practice of law; died in San Antonio, Texas, June 7.

•MAXEY, SAMUEL BELL, (1825-1895)- U. S. Senator, was born in Tomkinsville, Monroe County, Ky., March 30; attended the common schools, and was graduated from the United States Military Academy, West Point, N. Y., in 1846; served in the Mexican War until September 17, 1849, when he resigned and returned to Kentucky; studied law; was admitted to the bar in 1850 and commenced practice in Albany, Ky.; served as clerk of the county and circuit courts and as master in chancery 1852-1856; moved to Paris, Texas, in 1857 and practiced his profession; district attorney of Lamar County, Texas, in 1858 and 1859; elected to the State senate in 1861; but declined; during the Civil War raised the Ninth Regiment, Texas Infantry, of which he was colonel, for the Confederate Army; was promoted to the rank of brigadier general in 1862 and major general in 1864; commanded the Indian Territory military district 1863-1865 and was superintendent of Indian affairs; remained in the service until the surrender of the trans-Mississippi department May 26, 1865; resumed the practice of his profession in Paris, Texas; commissioned as judge of the eighth district of Texas April 18, 1873, but declined the position; elected as a Democrat to the United States Senate in 1875; reelected in 1881 and served from March 4, 1875, to March 3, 1887; was an unsuccessful candidate for reelection in 1887; continued the practice of law in Paris, Texas, until his death at Eureka Springs, Ark., August 16.

•MAYFIELD, EARLE BRADFORD, (1881-1964)- U. S. Senator, was born in Overton, Rusk County, Texas, April 12; attended the public schools in eastern Texas; was graduated from Southwestern University, Georgetown, Texas, in 1900; studied law at the University of Texas at Austin in 1900 and 1901; was admitted to the bar in 1907 and commenced practice in Meridian, Texas; also engaged in agricultural pursuits and in the wholesale grocery business; served in the States senate 1907-1913; member of the State railroad commission 1913-1923; delegate to the Democratic State conventions 1912-1948 and to the Democratic National Conventions at New York in 1924, at Houston in 1928, and at Chicago in 1932; elected as a Democrat to the United States

Senate and served from March 4, 1923, to March 3, 1929; unsuccessful candidate for renomination in 1928; in 1931 resumed the practice of law in Tyler, Texas, until retiring in 1952; died in Tyler, Texas, June 23.

•MCCLOSKEY, AUGUSTUS, (1878-1950)- U. S. Representative, was born in San Antonio, Bexar County, Texas, September 23; attended Atascosa (Texas) School, St. Joseph's Academy, San Antonio, Texas, and St. Mary's College, San Antonio, Texas; employed as a stenographer 1903-1907; studied law; was admitted to the bar in 1907 and commenced practice in San Antonio, Texas; judge of Bexar County 1920-1928; president of the Highway Club of Texas in 1926 and 1927; delegate to the Democratic National Convention at Houston, Texas, in 1928; presented credentials as a Democratic Member-elect the Seventy-first to Congress and served from March 4, 1929, to February 10, 1930, when he was succeeded by Harry M. Wurzbach, who successfully contested his election; was not a candidate for renomination in 1930; resumed the practice of law; judge of the corporation court of San Antonio, Texas, from January 1943 to July 1947; practiced law until his death in San Antonio, Texas, July 21.

•MCFARLANE, WILLIAM DODDRIDGE, (1894-1966)- U. S. Representative, was born in Greenwood, Sebastian County, Ark., July 17; attended the public schools and the University of Arkansas at Fayetteville 1900-1914; engaged in the mercantile business in Greenwood Ark., 1914-1918; during the First World War served as a private during training, was commissioned a second lieutenant in August 1918, and served until honorably discharged on December 13, 1918; returned to the University of Arkansas in 1919 and was graduated therefrom the same year with B. A. degree; Kent Law School, Chicago, Ill., LL. B., 1921, and J. D., 1969; was admitted to the bar in 1921 and commenced practice in Graham, Young County, Texas; member of the State house of representatives 1923-1927; served in the State senate 1927-1931; delegate to several Democratic State conventions; elected as a Democrat to the Seventy-third, Seventy-fourth, and Seventy-fifth Congresses (March 4, 1933-January 3, 1939); unsuccessful candidate for renomination in 1938; resumed the practice of law; special assistant to the attorney general at Texarkana, Texas, 1941-1944; director of the Surplus Property Smaller War Plants Corporation, Washington, D. C., from December 1944 to January 1946; special assistant to the Attorney General in Washington, D. C., January 1946 to July 1, 1951; unsuccessful candidate in 1951 to fill a vacancy in the Eighty-second Congress; with Lands Division, Justice Department, December 1, 1951.

•MCLEAN, WILLIAM PINKNEY, (1836-1925)- U. S. Representative, was born in Copiah County, Miss., August 9; moved with his mother to Marshall, Texas, in 1839; attended private schools until seventeen years of age, and was graduated from the law department of the University of North Carolina at Chapel Hill in 1857; was admitted to the bar in 1857 and commenced the practice of his profession at Jefferson, Marion County, Texas; member of the State house of representatives in 1861; resigned to enter the Confederate Army as a private; was promoted to captain and then major, and served throughout the Civil War; again a member of the State house of representatives in 1869; elected as a Democrat to the Forty-third Congress (March 4, 1873-March 3, 1875); was not a candidate for renomination in 1874; resumed the practice of law in Mount Pleasant, Titus County, Texas; member of the State constitutional convention in 1875; elected judge of the fifth judicial district in 1884; declined to be a candidate for reelection; appointed by Governor Hogg a member of the first State railroad commission in 1891; resigned and moved to Fort Worth, Tarrant County, Texas, in 1893; resumed the practice of his profession; died in Fort Worth on March 13.

•MCLEMORE, ATKINS JEFFERSON (JEFF), (1857-1929)-U. S. Representative, was born on a farm near Spring Hill, Maury County, Tenn., March 13; educated in the rural schools and by private tutors; moved to Texas in 1878; employed as a cowboy, printer, and newspaper reporter, and later as a miner in Colorado and Mexico; returned to Texas and settled in San Antonio and engaged principally in newspaper work; moved to Corpus Christi, Texas in 1889, to Austin 1895, and to Houston in 1911, where he engaged in the newspaper publishing business; member of the Texas House of Representatives of 1892-1896; member of the board of aldermen of Austin, Texas, 1896-1898; secretary of the Democratic State executive committee 1900-1904; elected as a Democrat to the Sixty-fourth and Sixty-fifth Congresses (March 4, 1915-March 3, 1919); was an unsuccessful candidate for reelection in 1918 to the Sixty-sixth Congress; resumed the newspaper publishing business in Hebronville, Jim Hogg County, Texas, and resided in Laredo, Texas; was an unsuccessful candidate for election to the United States Senate in 1928; died in Laredo, Texas, March 4.

•MEULLER, HAROLD (1920-), musician and .0educator, was born on January 28, 1920 in Austin, Texas. He received a bachelor's and Master's degree from the University of Michigan, and a Ph.D from the Eastman School of Music in Rochester, New York. Dr. Mueller served in USAAF from 1941 until 1946. After the war he was flutist with the Columbus Symphony orchestra, and the New Orleans Symphoney Orchestra. Following a post as instructor in the Eastman School of Music, he was assistant porfessor at the University of Minnesota, and professor and chairman of Austin College's music department. Dr. Mueller is a member and past chairman of the American Musicological Society, and the College Music Society. He is married and has two children.

•MILFORD, DALE, (1926-)- U. S. Representative, Democrat, of Grand Prairie, Texas; was born in Bug Tussle, Fannin County, February 18; son of Mr. and Mrs. Homer Dale Milford; veteran of World War II, serving as air traffic controller in Army Air Corps; post-war military duty, including service as Infantry and Signal Corps officer, Army pilot, and company commander; honorably discharged as captain, 1953; studied at Baylor University, Waco, Texas, 1953-57; began career in television weather-casting in 1953 in Waco, which continued until 1971 in Waco and Dallas; from 1963 to 1971 operated national consulting firm in meteorology and incorporation of weather radar techniques into television weather reporting; certified as "Professional Meterologist" by American Meteorological Society; lectured at Southern Methodist University, Dallas, on legal presentation of weather data; Lutheran; member of Aviation Advisory Committee of Skyline High School, Dallas; aerospace editor for WFAA-TV, Dallas, 1968-71; past member of board of directors of Dallas County Department of Public Welfare; member confederate Air Force Flying Museum; married to former Mary Michaelle Shattuck; two children: Steve and Shari; elected to 93d Congress, November 7, 1972.

•MILLER, JAMES FRANCIS, (1830-1902)- U. S. Representative, was born in Winnsboro, Fairfield District, S. C., August 1; moved with his parents to Texas in 1842; attended the common schools and Reutersville College; studied law; was admitted to the bar in 1857 and commenced practice in Gonzales, Texas; enlisted as a private in Company 1, Eighth Texas Cavalry, better known as "Terry's Texas Rangers," and served throughout the Civil War; resumed the practice of law in Gonzales, Texas; engaged in banking and stock raising; elected as a Democrat to the Forty-eighth and Forty-ninth Congresses (March 4, 1883-March 3, 1887); declined renomination; resumed former pursuits; elected as first president of the Texas Bankers' Association in 1885; died in Gonzales, Texas on July 3.

•**MILLS, ROGER QUARLES,** (1832-1911)- U. S. Representative and U. S. Senator, was born in Todd County, Ky., March 30; attended the common schools; moved to Texas in 1849; studied law; was admitted to the bar in 1852 and commenced practice in Corsicana, Texas; member of the State house of representatives in 1859 and 1860; enlisted in the Confederate Army, and served throughout the Civil War, attaining the rank of colonel of the Tenth Regiment, Texas Infantry; was wounded in the engagements at Missionary Ridge and Atlanta; elected as a Democrat to the Forty-third and to the nine succeeding Congresses and served from March 4, 1873, until his resignation on March 28, 1892, having been elected Senator; unsuccessful candidate for Speaker in the Fifty-second Congress; elected to the United States Senate to fill the vacancy caused by the resignation of John H. Reagan; reelected in 1893 and served from March 29, 1892, to March 3; died in Corsicana, Texas, September 2.

•**MOODY, DANIEL** (1893-1966), twenty-ninth governor of Texas (1927-31), was a native of Taylor, Texas, and the son of *Daniel and Nannie Robertson Moody.* His father was first mayor of Taylor, and sent his son to the new high school in town before he went to the University of Texas. He graduated from the university in 1914, with a degree in law. Young Daniel opened his own law office in Taylor in partnership with *Harris Melasky,* but when World War I broke out, he volunteered for service with the aviation section of the Army. He was commissioned second lieutenant with the Texas National Guard instead, and was stationed at Camp Pike, Arkansas. After the war, he worked as an attorney in Taylor and in 1920 was named County Attorney for Williamson County. In 1922-25, he was the District Attorney in his region, and in 1925 he was elected Attorney General of Texas. In that office he conducted an investigation of *Governor James Ferguson,* which resulted in a recovery of over $1 million from two contractors. He also defended Texas in boundary disputes with neighboring states at the U.S. Supreme Court. In 1926, he defeated incumbent *Miriam Ferguson,* and in 1927 was the youngest person ever to assume Texas governorship. Moody concentrated on reforms during his term; he approved a process of auditing state budgets, and reorganized the highway system and prison administration in the state. Moody was reelected for a second term in which he proved to be one of the most progressive governors in Texas history. He did not try for a third term, but returned to law at an office in Austin. He wanted to prevent Texas from repealing the Prohibition, but was unsuccessful. He was a special assistant to the U.S. Attorney General in the mid 1930s, but was never an elected official again. In 1948, he was not able to keep *Lyndon B. Johnson* off the Texas senatorial ballot, although the primary elections were questionable. He lived with his wife, the former, *Mildred Paxton*, in Austin until his death there.

•MOORE, JOHN MATTHEW, (1862-1940)- U. S. Representative, was born on a farm near Richmond, Fort Bend County, Texas, November 18; attended the common schools and the Agricultural and Mechanical College, College Station, Texas; engaged in mercantile pursuits, banking, stock raising, and farming; member of the State house of representatives 1896-1898; declined to be a candidate for renomination; delegate to the Democratic National Convention at Kansas City in 1900 and at St. Louis in 1916; elected as a Democrat to the Fifty-ninth Congress to fill the vacancy caused by the death of John M. Pinckney; reelected to the Sixtieth, Sixty-first, and Sixty-second Congresses and served from June 6, 1905, to March 3, 1913; was not a candidate for renomination in 1912; continued agricultural pursuits and stock raising near Richmond, Fort Bend County, Texas, until his death February 3.

•MOORE, LITTLETON WILDE, (1835-1911)- U. S. Representative, was born in Marion County, Ala., March 25; moved with his parents to Mississippi in 1836; was graduated from the University of Mississippi at Oxford in 1855; studied law and was admitted to the bar in 1857; moved to Texas in 1857; moved to Texas in 1857 and commenced practice in Bastrop; served as captain in the Confederate Army throughout the Civil war; elected to the State constitutional convention in 1875; district judge 1876-1885; elected as a Democrat to the Fiftieth, Fifty-first, and Fifty-second Congresses (March 4, 1887-March 3, 1893); resumed the practice of his profession; appointed judge of the twenty-second judicial district in 1901 and served until his death in Lagrange, Fayette County, Texas, October 29.

•MURRAH, PENDLETON (1824-1865), ninth governor of Texas (1863-65), was born in South Carolina, the son of unknown parents. He moved to Alabama as a young child and was educated by Baptist missionaries and finally at Brown University in Rhode Island. He studied law and was admitted to the Alabama bar, but soon afterwards settled in Harrison County, Texas where he made a reputation as a lawyer and orator. From the start, he took a prominent part in politics, and was in demand as a speaker at many public gatherings. Once, in opposition to the Know-Nothings, he was a candidate for Congress from his district, but was defeated. He was appointed to the Quartermaster's Department of the Confederate States Army in 1862, after having served the state legislature since 1857. In a nonpartisan, contest, Murrah won the governorship of Texas, still a Confederate state. The initial excitement over secession had died down, and farmers were beginning to wonder how they would survive, since all supplies were cut off from the North, and they were supposed to provide the large portion of supplies to all the South. A large part of the ammunition and other war articles were manufactured in Texas as well, principally at Huntsville and Austin. Murrah's term was full of difficulty, especially as most of the male population was off fighting the war, and the countryside was left without law enforcement. Upon the fall of the Confederacy in 1865, Murrah sought refuge in Mexico, where he died, at Monterrey, within two months.

N

•NEFF, PAT M. (1871-1952), twenty-seventh governor of Texas (1921-25), was born in McGregor, Texas, the son of *Noah and Isabel (Shepherd) Neff*, ranchers. He attended public school in Eagle Springs and then graduated from Baylor University in 1894 (M.A. 1898). The University of Texas gave him an L.L.B. degree in 1897 and soon he was admitted to the bar and was practicing law at Waco. He was elected to the state legislature in 1901 and became speaker in 1903 of the House. He was county attorney in McLennan County in 1906-12, trying over 400 cases. He was the first prosecutor in Texas to convict a man for allowing gambling and drinking in a prohibition area. A Democrat, Neff was elected governor after defeating political strongman *Joseph Baily* in the primary. Governor Neff founded the Texas Technological College, now Texas Tech. University and the South Texas State Teachers College, now Texas A & M University. In 1924 he set up the planning for Texas' centennial celebration, 12 years in advance of the event. He also abolished the Texas State Pardon Board. Riotous railroad strikes caused Neff to call martial law to Mexia as well as Limestone and Freestone Counties. Neff resumed his private law practice in 1925. Two years later *President Coolidge* appointed him to the National Board of Mediation. He was also on the Texas Railroad Commission in 1929-31. In 1932-47, Neff was President of Baylor University. He died of a heart attack in Waco.

135

•NIMITZ, CHESTER W. (1885-1966), World War II naval commander, was born in Fredericksburg, Texas to *Anna Henke and Chester B. Nimitz*. The family moved to Kerrville, Texas when he was a toddler. He dreamed of becoming a military officer at a young age and at 15 entered Annapolis Naval Academy. After graduation in 1905 he was assigned to the ship *Ohio*, which traveled from San Francisco to Manila and other Asian-Pacific seaports. Ensign Nimitz spent three years at sea, returned home, and then asked to be assigned to submarine duty, at a time when "under-sea crafts were regarded as a cross between *Jules Verne* fantasy and a whale." He commanded the *Plunger* in 1909-10, and then other subs, while quickly working his way up to lieutenant. In 1913, he studied diesel engine design in Germany and Belgium, and then supervised the construction of the U.S. Navy's first diesel-run ship. During World War I, Nimitz was made chief of staff for the Atlantic fleet submarine commander. His service merited a special Letter of Commendation from the Navy. He spent 1919-1922 at sea, and then studied at the Naval War College, which helped him gain an appointment on the staff of the U.S. Fleet Commander. Nimitz trained naval reserve officers at the University of California in 1926-29; it was the first such program in the Navy's history. By 1931, Nimitz had gained the title of Commander of the Submarine Division 12, and was in charge of several out-of-commission destroyers. The rest of the 1930s were spent in naval schools, and in the Navy's Bureau of Navigation, of which he was made Chief in 1939. When the Japanese bombed Pearl Harbor in 1941, Nimitz was named commander of the Pacific Fleet. After commanding an attack on *Midway* in 1942, he declared "Pearl Harbor has now been partially avenged. Vengeance will not be complete until Japanese sea power is reduced to impotence." In the next few years, Nimitz and his troops worked toward that end in a series of sea battles and island landings. In 1944, Nimitz was honored to be named Admiral of the fleet, a position created for him. Japan surrendered on Nimitzs' flagship on September 2, 1945. He returned home to work as Chief of Naval Operations for two years, and then as a special Assistant to the Secretary of the Navy. With *E.B. Potter*, he edited *Sea Power, A Naval History*, in 1960. He and his wife, the former *Catherine Freeman*, and four children, lived near San Francisco, California until his death.

•NOONAN, GEORGE HENRY, (1828-1907)- U. S. Representative; was born in Newark, N.J., August 20; received a liberal education; studied law; was admitted to the bar and practiced; moved to Texas in 1852 and settled in Castroville, Medina County; resumed the practice of law; elected judge of the eighteenth judicial district of Texas in 1862 and served until 1894 when he resigned; elected as a Republican to the Fifty-fourth Congress (March 4, 1895-March 3, 1897); unsuccessful candidate for reelection in 1896 to the Fifty-fifth congress; resumed the practice of law in San Antonio, Texas, and died there on August 17.

O

•OCHILTREE, THOMAS PECK, (1837-1902)- U. S. Representative, was born in Nacogdoches, Nacogdoches County, Texas, October 26; attended the public schools; volunteered in 1854 as a private in Capt. John G. Walker's company of Texas Rangers in the campaign against the Apache and Comanche Indians in 1854 and 1855; admitted to the bar by special act of the Texas Legislature in 1857; clerk of the State house of representatives 1856-1859; secretary of the State Democratic convention in 1859; editor of the Jeffersonian in 1860 and 1861; delegate to the Democratic National Conventions at Charleston, S. C., and Baltimore, Md., in 1860; during the Civil War enlisted in the Confederate Army in the First Texas Regiment and was promoted successively to lieutenant, captain, and major; served on the staffs of Generals Longstreet, Taylor, Green, and Maxey; editor of the Houston Daily Telegraph 1866 and 1867; appointed commissioner of immigration for Texas in Europe 1870-1873; appointed United States marshal for the eastern district of Texas by President Grant January 8, 1874; elected as an Independent to the Forty-eighth Congress (March 4, 1883-March 3, 1885); moved to New York City, N. Y. and retired from public and political activities; died at Hot Springs, Bath County, Va., on November 25.

•O'DANIEL, WILBER LEE (1890-1969), thirty-third governor of Texas (1939-41), was born in Malta, Ohio to *William Barnes and Alice Thompson O'Daniel.* He attended public schools after the family moved to Arlington, Kansas, and he studied at a business college in Hutchinson. He became involved with a flour-milling company, eventually rising to executive levels. O'Daniel was most known for his radio work in Texas; he gave a noontime music and humor show with the "Light Crust Doughboys."

Although this may have been a ploy to sell more of his company's flour, O'Daniel's humor and down-home advice brought in many listeners in Texas. He also wrote "Beautiful Texas", now the state song. He was not an active politician, but entered the Democratic primary for governor in 1938. Soon, people took notice of his promises of better old-age pensions and an accessible administration. O'Daniel did retain his "down home" demeanor in office, but wasn't able to increase in old-age funds. His inexperience in government made him less than effectual at times. However, he had strong support from the public, who saw him as someone who had beaten the odds and defied the powerful rich. That O'Daniel was also a shrewd businessman and a good actor had little bearing on the opinion of the voters, and he was reelected by a large majority in 1940. When *Morris Sheppard* died and his U.S. Senate seat was empty, O'Daniel successfully ran to take his place. He resigned the governorship in August, 1941. After a second term that ended in 1949, he returned to Austin and remained a public figure despite his failure to win the governor's seat in 1956 and 1958. He died at Austin.

•ORTIZ, SOLOMON PORFIRIO, (1938-)- U. S. Representative, Democrat, of Corpus Christi, Texas; was born in Robstown, June 3; graduated, Robstown High School, 1955; Del Mar College, Corpus Christi; officers certificate, Institute of Applied Science, Chicago, Ill., 1962; officer's certificate, National Sheriffs' Training Institute, Los Angeles, Calif., 1977; served in U.S. Army, specialist 4th class, 1960-62; insurance agent; Nueces County constable, 1965-68; Nueces County commissioner, 1969-76; Nueces County sheriff, 1977-82; member: Sheriffs' Association of Texas, National Sheriffs' Association; honors: Man of the Year, International Order of Foresters, 1981; two children: Yvette and Solomon, Jr.; elected on November 2, 1982 to the 98th Congress.,

P

•PARKER, CYNTHIA ANN (1827-1864?), Indian captive, was born in Illinois, but moved to Comanche Country near the present Groesbeck, Texas while still a child. In 1836, Indians attacked the fort in which she lived, killing several people and taking captives, among them the young Parker. The Quahada tribe then adopted her and trained her in the Indian ways. She adjusted so well that she married an important war chief, *Naconah*, and gave birth to two sons and a daughter. Although she might have been recaptured by whites two times, she repelled them, and it wasn't until she was forcibly taken by a group of Texas Rangers in 1860 that she again lived with her own race. At the time of her capture, she appeared as dark-skinned as the Indians, (although her hair was blonde) and remembered no English except her name. She was never happy after returning to her brother's home north of Tyler, and when the only child she took with her died, she was not long in following. Parker's oldest son, *Quanah*, lived on to become one of the fiercest Comanche war chiefs. Later, he settled in Oklahoma, and had his mother's remains transferred from her grave in Henderson County, Texas to a plot near his home at Fort Sill.

•PARRISH, LUCIAN WALTON, (1878-1922)- U. S. Representative, was born in Sister Grove, near Van Alstyne, Grayson County, Texas, January 10; moved with his parents to Clay County in 1887 and settled near Joy, Texas; attended the public schools of Joy and Bowie, Texas, and the North Texas State Normal College at Denton, Texas; taught school for two years; was graduated from the law department of the University of Texas at Austin in 1909; was admitted to the bar the same year and com-

141

menced practice in Henrietta, Texas; elected as a Democrat to the Sixty-sixth and Sixty-seventh Congresses and served from March 4, 1919, until his death in Wichita Falls, Wichita County, Texas, March 27.

•PASCHAL, THOMAS MOORE, (1845-1919)- U. S. Representative, was born in Alexandria, Rapides Parish, La., December 15; moved with his parents to San Antonio, Texas, in 1846; educated in private schools; attended St. Mary's College, San Antonio, Texas; was graduated from Centre College, Danville, Ky., in 1866; studied law; was admitted to the bar in 1867 and commenced practice in San Antonio; city attorney in 1867; United States commissioner for the western district of Texas 1867-1869; judge of the district criminal court for San Antonio in 1870 and 1871; moved to Castroville, Texas, in 1870; district attorney of the twenty-fourth district 1871-1875; moved to Brackett, King County, in 1873; elected judge of the thirty-eighth judicial district in 1876; reelected in 1880 and 1884, and served until 1892; appointed by Governor Coke as extradition agent between the United States and Mexico in 1876 and reappointed by Governor Roberts in 1880; returned to Castroville in 1885; elected as a Democrat to the Fifty-third Congress (March 4, 1893-March 3, 1895); unsuccessful candidate for renomination in 1894; resumed the practice of law in San Antonio, Texas; delegate to the Democratic National Convention at Chicago in 1896; died in New York City, January 28.

•PATMAN, WILLIAM N., (1927-)- U. S. Representative, Democrat, of Ganado, Texas; was born in Texarkana, March 26; son of the late Congressman and Mrs. Wright Patman; attended the Texarkana and Washington, D.C., public schools; Eagle Scout; graduated, Kemper Military School, Boonville, Mo., 1944; B.B.A., 1953; LL.B., 1953, University of Texas; enlisted at age 17 and served as private first class, U.S. Marine Corps, 1945-46; captain, USAF Reserve, 1953-66; diplomatic courier, U.S. Foreign Service, 1949-50; legal examiner, oil and gas division, Texas Railroad Commission, 1953-55; admitted to the Texas State Bar in 1953 and commenced private practice in Ganado, 1955; city attorney, Ganado, 1955-60; member, Texas State Senate, 1961-81; Society for Range Management, Award of Excellence, 1975; charter member, Ganado Jaycees; former president, Jackson County United Fund; chairman, official board, First Methodist Church; and Rotarian; member: Texas and American Bar Association, Texas and Southwestern and Independent Cattle Raisers Association, Phi Alpha Delta, Delta Sigma Pi, Sigma Alpha Epsilon, Scabbard and Blade, American Legion; married to the former Carrin Mauritz, 1953; one daughter, Carrin Foreman Patman; elected to the 97th Congress, November 4, 1980.

•PATMAN, WRIGHT, (1893-)- U. S. Representative, was born at Patman's Switch near Hughes Springs, Cass County, Texas, August 6; attended the public schools; was graduate from Hughes Springs (Texas) High School in 1912 and from the law department of Cumberland University, Lebanon, Tenn., in 1916; engaged in agricultural pursuits in Texas in 1913 and 1914; was admitted to the bar in 1916 and commenced practice in Hughes Springs, Texas; assistant county attorney of Cass County, Texas in 1916 and 1917; during the First World War served as a private and later as a machine-gun officer in the United States Army 1917-1919; member of the State house of representatives, United States Senate and served from March 4, 1867, to March 3, 1873; Regent of the Smithsonian Institution; again a member of the State house of representatives in 1877 and 1878; State superintendent of public instruction 1885-1893; president of American Institute of Instruction; died in Hanover, N. H.,on May 4; interment in Dartmouth Cemetery.

•PATTON, NAT, (1884-1957)- U. S. Representative, was born on a farm near Tadmor, Houston County, Texas, February 26; attended the rural schools and Sam Houston Normal School, Huntsville; Texas; taught in the rural and high schools 1899-1918; also engaged in agricultural pursuits at Belott, Houston County,

Texas, in 1915 and 1916; member of the State house of representatives in 1912 and 1913; attended the law department of the University of Texas at Austin; was admitted to the bar in 1918 and commenced practice in Crockett, Houston County, Texas; served as county judge of Houston County, Texas, 1918-1922; member of the State senate 1929-1934; delegate to the Democratic State convention at Beaumont in 1924 and at Fort Worth in 1935; during the First World War enlisted in the United States Army on November 1, 1918, but was never sworn in due to the armistice being signed; was commissioned a first lieutenant in the Intelligence Department but did not report for duty; elected as a Democrat to the Seventy-fourth and to the four succeeding Congresses (January 3, 1935-January 3, 1945); unsuccessful candidate for renomination in 1944; resumed the practice of law; died in Crockett, Texas, July 27.

•PAUL, RON, (1935-)- U. S. Representative, Republican, of Lake Jackson, Texas; was born August 20; B.A., Gettysburg College, Gettysburg, Pa., 1957; M.D., Duke University Medical Center, Durham, N.C., 1961; served in the U.S. Air Force, captain, flight surgeon, 1963-65; physician and obstetrician-gynecologist; married to the former Carol Wells, 1957; five children: Ronald, Lori, Randal, Robert, and Joy; elected to the 94th Congress in a special election, April 3, 1976; unsuccessful candidate for reelection to the 95th Congress; resumed the practice of his profession; elected to the 96th Congress, November 7, 1978; reelected to the 97th and 98th Congresses.

•PEASE, ELISHA M. (1812-83), fourth and twelfth governor of Texas (1853-57 and 1867-70), was born in Enfield, Connecticut, the son of *Lorain and Sarah Marshall Pease.* He attended local public schools and an academy in Westfield, Massachussetts before working as a clerk in a country store at the age of 14. He visited New Orleans in 1834, and was determined to make his home in the West, so he moved to the frontier country of Texas and studied with a lawyer in present-day Bastrop. In late 1835 he joined the Texas Revolutionary movement, participating in the first battle of the war at Gonzales. Soon afterward he was made secretary of the provisional government council, where he served until early 1836, when the interim government intervened. He was then successively chief clerk of the navy and treasury departments, and acted as secretary of the treasury until a replacement could be found for the deceased *Bailey Hardeman.* He also practiced law at Brazoria in 1837-46. In 1845, when Texas was annexed to the U.S., Pease was elected to represent his county in the first state legislature. During his two terms he drew up nearly all the laws, defining the jurisdiction of the courts and securing the enactment of the 1848 probate laws. He was a state senator for a short while, got married, and was elected governor in 1853. Pease emphasized growth during his first term, supporting the construction of railroads, a state university, a new capitol building, and state institutions for the deaf, dumb and insane. He won a second term in 1855, but declined a third term. He was strongly opposed to secession during the Civil War and lived as a recluse until the end of it, when he was elected a delegate from Texas to the convention of southern loyalists in 1866. He was appointed provisional governor of Texas by *General Griffin* in 1867, when *Throckmorton* was removed as "an impediment to Reconstruction." Pease resigned two years later when *Griffin* was replaced by *General Reynolds,* and retired to private law practice in Austin. He was a member of the Liberal Republican Convention of 1872. In 1879 he accepted his last public office, as the collector of the port of Galveston. He died while vacationing at a spa in Lampasas Springs, Texas.

•PENDLETON, GEORGE CASSETY, (1845-1913)- U. S. Representative, was born near Viola, Warren County, Tenn., April 23; attended the country schools and the Hannah High School; moved with his parents to Ellis County, Texas, in 1857; settled in Belton, Texas, and engaged in mercantile and agricultural pursuits; during the Civil War entered the Confederate service as a private in Captain Forrest's Company, Watson's Regiment, Parson's Brigade, Texas Cavalry; at the close of the war attended Waxahachie Academy in Ellis County, Texas;

employed as a commercial traveler for twelve years; engaged in mercantile and agricultural pursuits; delegate to every Democratic State convention from 1876 to 1910; member of the State house of representatives 1882-1888 and served as speaker in 1886; Lieutenant Governor of Texas 1890-1892; delegate to the Democratic National Convention at Chicago in 1896; elected as a Democrat to the Fifty-third and Fifty-fourth Congresses (March 4, 1893-March 3, 1897); declined to be a candidate for renomination in 1896; engaged in banking in Temple, Bell County, Texas; studied law; was admitted to the bar in 1900 and practiced in Temple until his death there on January 19.

•PICKETT, THOMAS AUGUSTUS (TOM), (1906-)- U. S. Representative, was born in Travis, Falls County, Texas, August 14; attended the public schools of Palestine, Texas, and the University of Texas at Austin; studied law; was admitted to the bar in 1929 and commenced practice in Palestine, Texas; county attorney of Anderson County 1931-1935; district attorney of the third judicial district of Texas 1935-1945; elected as a Democrat to the Seventy-ninth and to the three succeeding Congresses and served from January 3, 1945, until his resignation June 30, 1952; vice president of the National Coal Association from July 1, 1952, to March 31, 1961; vice president of the Association of American Railroads, April 1, 1961, to November 30, 1967; is a resident of Leesburg, Fla.

•PICKLE J.J. (JAKE), (1913-)- U. S. Representative, Democrat, of Austin, Texas; was born October 11 in Roscoe, Nolan County, son of J. B. and Mary Pickle; educated in public schools of Big Spring, Texas; graduate of the University of Texas, B.A. degree; area director, National Youth Administration, 1938-41, resigning to enter Navy during W.W. II, serving 3 1/2 years in Pacific; after discharge from Navy entered radio business as one of coorganizers of Radio Station KVET, Austin, Texas; later entered public relations and advertising business; director of Texas State Democratic Executive Committee 1957-60; appointed member Texas Employment Commission in 1961, resigning September 27, 1963, to be candidate for the Congress; elected in special election December 17, 1963, to the 88th Congress; reelected to the 89th, 90th, 91st, 92d, and 93d Congresses; married the former Beryl Bolton McCarroll; three children, Mrs. James Norris, Dick McCarroll, and Graham McCarroll.

•PILSBURY, TIMOTHY, (1789-1858)- U. S. Representative, was born in Newburyport, Mass., April 12; attended the common schools; employed in a store for about two years; became a sailor and during the War of 1812 commanded the privateer Yankee; engaged in shipping; settled in Eastport, Maine; member of the Maine House of Representatives in 1825 and 1826; member of the executive council 1827-1836; unsuccessful candidate for election in 1836 to the Twenty-fifth Congress; moved to Ohio, thence to New Orleans, La., and later to Brazoria, Texas; member of the house of representatives of the Republic of Texas in 1840 and 1841 and served in the senate of that Republic in 1842; chief justice of the county court; judge of probate for Brazoria County; again a member of the Texas Senate in 1845; upon the admission of Texas as a State into the Union was elected as a Calhoun Democrat to the Twenty-ninth and Thirtieth Congresses and served from March 30, 1846, to March 3, 1849; unsuccessful candidate for reelection in 1848 to the Thirty-first Congress; died in Henderson, Rusk County, Texas, November 23.

•PINCKNEY, JOHN MCPHERSON, (1845-1905)- U. S. Representative, was born in Grimes County, Texas, near the town of Hempstead, Waller County, May 4; attended the public schools and was privately instructed; enlisted as a private in the Confederate Army and served in company D, Fourth Texas Brigade, until the close of the Civil War, attaining the rank of first lieutenant; studied law; was admitted to the bar in 1875 and commenced practice in Hempstead, Texas; district attorney for the twenty-third judicial district of Texas 1890-1900; voluntarily retired; county judge of Waller County 1900-1903; elected as a Democrat to the Fifty-ninth Congress and served from November 17, 1903, until April 214.

•**POAGE, WILLIAM ROBERT,** (1899-)- U. S. Representative, was born in Waco, McLennan County, Texas, December 28; in 1901 moved to Throckmorton County, Texas, with his parents, who settled near Woodson; attended the rural schools of Throckmorton County, Texas; during the First World War served as an apprentice seaman in the United States Navy; attended the University of Texas at Austin and the University of Colorado at Boulder; Baylor University, Waco, Texas, A. B., 1921; engaged in agricultural pursuits 1920-1922; instructor in geology at Baylor University 1922-1924; law department of Baylor University, LL. B., 1924; was admitted to the bar the same year and commenced practice in Waco, Texas; instructor in law at Baylor University 1924-1928; member of the State house of representatives 1925-1929; served in the State senate 1931-1937; delegate, Texas State Democratic Convention, 1922; delegate, Democratic National Conventions, 1956, 1960, and 1964; elected as a Democrat to the Seventy-fifth and to the sixteen succeeding Congresses (January 3, 1937-January 3, 1971). Reelected to the Ninety-second Congress.

•**POOL, JOE RICHARD,** (1911-1968)- U. S. Representative, was born in Fort Worth, Tarrant County, Texas, February 18; attended the Dallas public schools and Tecas University, 1929-1933; graduated from Southern Methodist University School of Law, Dallas, Texas, in 1937; was admitted to the Texas bar the same year and commenced the practice of law in Dallas, Texas; served with the United States Army as a special investigator, Air Corps Intelligence, 1943-1945; member of State house of representatives, 1953-1958; elected as a Democrat to the Eighty-eighth, Eighty-ninth, and Ninetieth Congresses, serving from January 3, 1963, until his death in Houston, Texas, July 14.

•**PORTER, WILLIAM SYDNEY (O. HENRY)** (1862-1910), author, derived many of the settings for his stories from Texas. He was born in Greensboro, North Carolina to *Algernon and Mary Jane Swain Porter*, who died when he was a young boy. He lived with an aunt for a few years, and since he was sickly, learned to love reading as a pastime. While working in his uncle's store, he would read stories to the customers. Eventually, the stories he read were his own. Young William's ill health caused his father to send him to a ranch in Texas when he was 19. There, he took up odd jobs in the country, and in town. In his twenties, Porter wrote for the Houston *Post* as a reporter, and also published a humor newspaper, which he called the *Rolling Stone*. In these positions, he gained much of his experience in writing about life in the city. In 1891-94, he worked for a drug store and bank in Austin. When he was accused of stealing money from the bank Porter fled to Honduras, and worked on a banana plantation until he received word that his wife was ill. She died soon after he returned to Austin to visit her. The police then caught him and he was convicted with embezzling the bank's money. While serving out his five year sentence, Porter began writing short stories and sending them to several magazines. He used the pseudonym "O. Henry" for the first time while in prison. Porter moved to New Orleans and then to New York City when his time was up, and decided to pursue writing for a living. The cities fascinated him, especially New York, which he called "Baghdad of the Subway." At first, he was not successful at making this living; *The Emancipation of Billy* was rejected 17 times before it was published and acclaimed by the critics. Afterwards, he published such stories as *Cabbages and Kings " The Voice of the City* and *The Heart of the West,* all sentimental tales of everyday people in large cities or in Texas. His style has been described as "episodic," since he deals in short, ironic, or otherwise unusual scenes in the lives of people who might be considered insignificant in a complex society. His *Gift of the Magi* is a good example of this insight; it has been a favorite Christmas story since its publication. Many of his tales also feature Texas Rangers, sheriffs, cowboys, outlaws and other Western characters that Porter learned about in Texas. His *A Departmental Case* is an outstanding example of these stories. After 1904, O. Henry's stories had begun to be collected in book form. His last book, *Whirligigs*, was published in 1910, but many more were published posthumously. His works are favorites for anthologies of short stories. O. Henry has been called "the greatest master of the short story in America except possibly for *Poe. "* He was married a second time, in 1907, to *Sara Lindsay*, and left one daughter from the first marriage when he died.

•**PRICE, ROBERT DALE (BOB)**, (1927-)- U. S. Representative, Republican, of Pampa, Texas; was born September 7; Reading, Kansas, son of Ben F. Price, Sr., and Gladys Ann Price; educated in the public schools of Reading, Kansas; received Bachelor of Science degree from Oklahoma State University, 1951; married Martha Ann (Marty) White, daughter of Mr. and Mrs. Carl White of Oklahoma City, Okla., 1951; three children -Robert Grant, Benjamin Carl, and Janice Ann; served 4 years active duty in U.S. Air Force as a Sabre jet fighter pilot; flew 27 combat missions during the Korean conflict; awarded Air Medal; returned to Texas Panhandle after honorable discharge in 1955; rancher; owns ranch in Texas; Baptist; board of development, Wayland Baptist College; Mason, Top o' Texas Lodge No. 1381; Shriner, Khiva Temple; United States Air Force Association; American Legion; Veterans of Foreign Wars; past president, Top o' Texas Kiwanis Club; Pampa Chamber of Commerce; West Texas Chamber of Commerce; former chairman, Gray County Airport Board; Texas and Southwestern Cattle Raisers Association; honorary director, Top o' Texas Rodeo, Horse Show and Fair Association, Inc.; former district organization and extension chairman, Boy Scouts of America; Sigma Alpha Episilon fraternity; Okalhoma State University Alumni Association; elected to the 90th Congress November 8, 1966; reelected to 91st, 92d, and 93d Congresses; member, Agriculture Committee, Livestock and Feed Grains Subcommittee, Cotton Subcommittee, and ranking minority member on Department Operations Subcommittee; House Armed Services Committee, Subcommittee on Research and Development; member, House Republican Policy Committee; former president 90th Club; home address; R.R.1, Box 61-A, or Box 2476, Pampa, Texas.

•PURCELL, GRAHAM, (1919-)- U. S. Representative, Democrat, of Wichita Falls, Texas; son of Graham B. Purcell and Della Key Purcell; born in Archer City, on May 5; attended public schools in Archer City; graduated Texas A. & M. College with a B.S. degree in agriculture in 1946; received LL.B. degree from Baylor Universitiy Law School in 1949; entered United States Army in 1941; served in Africa and Italy; remained in the Active Reserves, now lieutenant colonel, Armor, U.S.A.R.; married in 1970 to Nancy Putty; four children by former marriage: Blaine, Kirk, Blake, and Jannie; practicing attorney in Big Spring, Texas, and Wichita Falls, Texas, from 1949 until 1955; appointed judge of the 89th Judicial District of Texas in 1955; reelected twice to that position in Wichita County; also served as juvenile court judge of Wichita County; very active in work with juveniles, both as judge and civic worker; district chairman, Boy Scouts of America; honored twice as "Outstanding Citizen of Wichita Falls"; deacon in Fain, Memorial Presbyterian Church of Wichita Falls; elected to 87th Congress in special election, January 27, 1962, from the 13th Congressional District of Texas; reelected to the 88th, 89th, 90th, 91st, and 92d Congresses; appointed to National Commission on Food Marketing by Speaker of the House on July 20, 1964; member, House Committee on Agriculture since 1962; past chairman Wheat Subcommittee; presently chairman Livestock and Grains Subcommittee; member of Post Office and Civil Service Committee of the House.

R

•RANDELL, CHOICE BOSWELL, (1857-1945)- (nephew of Lucius Jeremiah Gartrell)- U. S. Representative, was born near Spring Place, Murray County, Ga., January 1; attended public and private schools and the North Georgia Agricultural College at Dahlonega; studied law; was admitted to the bar in 1878 and commenced practice in Denison, Grayson County, Texas, in January 1879; moved to Sherman, Texas, in 1882 and continued the practice of law; elected as a Democrat to the Fifty-seventh and to the five succeeding Congresses (March 4, 1901-March 3, 1913); unsuccessful candidate for nomination to the United States Senate in 1912; resumed the practice of law; died in Sherman, Texas, October 19.

•RAYBURN, SAMUEL T. (1882-1961), former Speaker of the U.S. House of Representatives, was born in Roane County, Tennessee, but grew up on a farm near Bonham, Texas. He picked cotton for a living with the rest of the family until he was 17 and went to school at East Texas Normal College. With the help of various odd jobs, Rayburn was able to finish his B.S. degree in 1903. He taught school for a time, but soon pursued his main ambition--to win a seat in the state legislature. "With a pony, a smile, and determination," his campaigning worked, and he was soon in Austin working on legislation. In the meantime, he worked on a law degree from the University of Texas, which he recieved in 1908. At that time, he returned to Bonham to practice, but kept his seat in the legislature, becoming house speaker in 1911. The next year he was elected to the House of Representatives. Rayburn had dreamed of being speaker of that body since he had heard *Senator Joseph Weldon Bailey* speak in 1894. Rayburn got his dream in 1937, and retained that seat for 24 years, except when

153

Republicans dominated the House in 1947-49 and 1953-55. Rayburn served one of the longest terms on record in the House; he was reelected a total of 24 times, or 48 years and eight months, and "Mr. Sam" had a warm personality, was patriotic, and knew the legislative process well, which made him many friends in both parties. He was a friend to Presidents *Roosevelt, Truman, Eisenhower* and *Kennedy.* Texans, especially in the northern part of the state, venerate Rayburn as a national hero. His Washington office has been recreated in a special museum at Bonham.

•REAGAN, JOHN HENNINGER, (1818-1905)- U. S. Representative and U. S. Senator, was born in Sevierville, Sevier County, Tenn., October 8; attended the common schools, Nancy Academy, Boyds Creek Academy, and Maryville Academy, Maryville, Tenn.; joined the Army and participated in campaigns against the Cherokee Indians; deputy surveyor of the public lands 1839-1843; studied law; was admitted to the bar in 1846 and practiced in Buffalo and Palestine, Texas; member of the State house of representatives 1847-1849; judge of the district court from 1852 to 1857, when he resigned; elected as a Democrat to the Thirty-fifth and Thirty-sixth Congresses (March 4, 1857-March 3, 1861); elected to the seccession convention of Texas in 1861; deputy to the Provisional Congress of the Confederacy; appointed Postmaster General of the Confederacy March 6, 1861; reappointed in 1862 and occupied the position until the close of the war; member of the State constitutional convention in 1875; elected as a Democrat to the Forty-fourth and to the five succeeding Congresses (March 4, 1875-March 3, 1887); had been reelected to the Fiftieth Congress but resigned March 4, 1887, to become Senator; elected to the United States Senate and served from March 4, 1887, until June 10, 1891, when he resigned; returned to Texas and was appointed a member of the railroad commission of the State and served as chairman 1897-1903; died in Palestine, Anderson County, Texas, March 6.

•REGAN, KENNETH MILLS, (1893-1959)- U. S. Representative, was born in Mount Morris, Ogle County, Ill., March 6; attended the public schools and Vincennes (Ind.) University; during the First World War served as a flyer in the United States Army Signal Corps; in 1920 engaged in the real estate business and as an oil operator in Pecos, Texas; alderman of the city of Pecos; mayor of Pecos 1929-1932; member of the State senate 1933-1937; in World War II served as an intelligence officer in the Air Corps and was discharged with the rank of captain; moved to Midland, Texas, and continued oil operations; elected as a Democrat to the Eightieth Congress to fill the vacancy caused by the resignation of Robert Ewing Thomason; reelected to the Eighty-first, Eighty-second, and Eighty-third Congresses, and served from August 23, 1947, to January 3, 1955;unsuccessful candidate for renomination in 1954 to the Eighty-fourth congress; representative of Texas railroads in Washington, D. C.; died in Santa Fe, N. Mex., on August 15.

•ROBERTS, HERBERT RAY, (1913-)- U. S. Representative, was born in Collin County, near McKinney, Texas, March 28; graduated from McKinney High School; attended Texas A. & M. University, North Texas State, and University of Texas; served on the staff of Speaker Sam Rayburn of the House of Representataives, Washington, D. C., 1941-1942; during World War II entered active duty in the United States Navy as a lieutenant (jg.) serving from 1942 to 1945; was aboard the aircraft U.S.S. Hornet lost in action, 1942, subsequently commanded U.S.S. LST-335 in invasions of Sicily and Salerno, Italy, and Normandy, France; recalled to active duty in the Korean conflict; now holds rank of captain, United States Naval Reserve; businessman with diversified interests including farming; served in the State senate, 1955-1962, and was president pro tempore, 1961, regular session; elected as a Democrat in special election to the Eighty-seventh Congress to fill the vacancy caused by the death of Sam Rayburn; reelected to the four succeeding Congresses, and served from January 30, 1962, to January 3, 1971. Reelected to the Ninety-second Congress.

•**ROBERTS, ORAN M.** (1815-1898), sixteenth governor of Texas (1879-83), was born in Laurens, South Carolina to *Oba and Margaret Ewing Roberts*. When his father died, he lived with his mother in Ashville, Alabama, and managed a plantation while going to school part-time. He also received private tutoring before studying at the University of Alabama. He graduated from there in 1836 and studied law for one year more. He practiced with lawyers in Talladega and Ashville, Alabama and was a representative in the state legislature before moving to San Augustine, Texas in 1841. He was appointed district attorney for his area in 1844, where he dealt in tax and import laws. He soon became convinced that the only fair tax on property was *ad valorem*, and his principles were eventually incorporated into the laws of Texas. *Governor Henderson* appointed Roberts a district judge for the Fifth District in 1846. He resigned to practice law privately, but in 1857 he was once again in the public eye when he was elected an associate justice of the state supreme court. He was a staunch states rights Democrat and an ardent advocate of secession. He was a colonel in the Civil War, fighting in Louisiana. He was displaced after the war from his position of chief justice of the state supreme court in 1864-65 but was again the chief in 1874-78. In 1866 he was elected a member from Smith County to the state constitutional convention and the same year was chosen by the legislature to become a U.S. Senator, but was not allowed to take his seat. In 1868-70 he was a professor of law and agriculture at a high school in Gilmer, Texas. In 1878 he was elected governor, and reelected in 1880. State taxes were reduced in his administration from 50 to 30 cents on $100, but he was able to leave the treasury with a $500,000 surplus by the end of his term. Public schools were improved, and two Normal schools were established, one for whites and one for blacks. The State University at Austin was also organized and built during his terms. Two transcontinental railroads were completed in the state. He also supervised the plans for a new capitol building to be built over the spot where the old one had burned in 1881. Declining a third nomination on account of failing health, Roberts returned to his country house, but soon afterwards began a professorship of law at the University of Texas at Austin, where he remained until retirement in 1893. He was the author of *A Description of Texas*, 1881; *The Elements of Texas Pleading,*

1890; *Our Federal Relations, from a Southern View of Them,* 1895; he also coedited *Clement Evans' Confederate Military History.* He had been president of the Texas Historical Society in 1874 and was a Mason. Roberts died at his home at Marble Falls, on the Colorado River northwest of Austin.

•ROGERS, WALTER EDWARD, (1908-)- U. S. Representative, was born in Texarkana, Miller County, Ark., July 19; attended the public schools in McKinney, Texas; attended Austin College, Sherman, Texas, in 1926, and the law school of the University of Texas at Austin until 1935; was admitted to the bar in 1935 and commenced the practice of law in 1936 in Pampa, Texas; city attorney of Pampa 1938-1940; district attorney of the thirty-first judicial district of Texas, 1943-1947; delegate to Texas State Democratic Conventions, 1950-1956, and 1960; delegate to National Democratic Conventions from 1952 to 1964; elected as a Democrat to the Eighty-second and to the seven succeeding Congresses (January 3, 1951-January 3, 1967); was not a candidate for reelection in 1966 to the Ninetieth Congress; resumed the practice of law; president, Independent Natural Gas Association of America; is a resident of Chevy Chase, Md.

•ROSS, LAWRENCE S. (1838-1898), eighteenth governor of Texas (1887-91), was a native of Bentonsport, Iowa, the son of *Shapley Prince,* an Indian fighter and agent, and *Catherine Fulkerson Ross.* The family moved to Austin, Texas in 1846 and young Lawrence attended public schools until his entrance to Baylor University at Waco. He continued his education at Wesleyan University in Florence, Alabama, from which he graduated in 1859. That year, he also married *Elizabeth Tinsley* and returned to Texas, where he followed his father's example by fighting Comanche Indians along the Pease River with the Texas Rangers. *Governor Houston* made him an aide-de-camp of the state troops, with the rank of colonel. Ross joined the Confederate Army in 1861, beginning as a private and rising to the rank of brigadier general by 1864. He fought in Mississippi and Georgia, 135 battles in all. He returned to Texas and led a quiet life until

1873 when he was elected sheriff of McLennan County. He was a delegate to the Texas Constitutional Convention of 1875. In 1881-83 he was a member of the state senate, serving as chair of the committee on finance, and being nominated for governor in 1886, he was elected by a large majority. Ross was a popular governor, especially since times were getting better in Texas. Railroads were built rapidly; taxes were reduced; immigration was promoted by societies established to attract settlers, and the U.S. government paid into the state treasury nearly $1 million for expenses incurred by the state in defending its borders since annexation in 1846. In May 1888 the new state capitol was dedicated, and new reformatories and asylums were built at that time. Ross also approved new regulations for railroad companies and supported an amendment to the state constitution for prohibition of alcohol. That amendment failed with the voters. Ross left office without trying for a third term, and soon was appointed President of the new Texas Agricultural and Mechanical College at Bryan. He was offered a place on the State Railroad Commission, but turned it down in favor of remaining at the college. He held the post until his death, and was buried at Waco.

•RUNNELS, HARDIN R. (1820-1873), fifth governor of Texas (1857-59), was born in Mississippi. His father was *Hardin D. Runnels*, but his mother and any sisters and brothers are unrecorded. He went to Texas in 1841 and located on a cotton plantation along the Red River in Bowie County. In 1847-53, he was a representative from his county in the state legislature, and in 1855 he was elected lieutenant governor of the state on the Democratic ticket. Runnels defeated *Sam Houston*, who was suffering temporary unpopularity because of his stance on the Missouri Compromise, for governor in 1857. During his administration, Governor Runnels opposed large state grants to railroad companies and built up the state militia. However, Indian raids continued to terrorize the new settlers in Texas, and Runnels was not favored in the next election because of his inability to stop them. He retired to his plantation after 1859, and was strongly active in politics in 1861, at the secession convention, and at the constitutional convention of 1866. He is credited with founding the state Historical Association. He died at home.

•**RUSK, THOMAS JEFFERSON,** (1803-1857)U. S. Senator, was born in Pendleton District, S. C.; completed preparatory studies; studied law; was admitted to the bar and commenced practice in Georgia; moved to Nacogdoches, Texas, in 1835; delegate to the convention which declared for the independence of Texas March 21, 1836; first Secretary of War of the new Republic; at the Battle of San Jacinto took command of the forces after General Houston was wounded and retained command until October 1836, when he resumed his duties as Secretary of War; member of the Second Congress of the Republic of Texas; chief justice of the supreme court of Texas 1838-1842; appointed brigadier general of militia of the Republic of Texas in 1843; president of the convention that confirmed the annexation of Texas to the United States in 1845; upon the admission of Texas as a State into the Union was elected as a Democrat to the United States Senate; reelected in 1851 and 1857 and served from February 21, 1846, until his death; was elected President pro tempore of the Senate on March 14, 1857, in the special session of the Senate; died in Nacogdoches, Tex., July 29.

•**RUSSELL, GORDON JAMES,** (1859-1915)- U.S. Representative, was born in Huntsville, Madison County, Ala.; attended the common schools, the Sam Bailey Institute, Griffin, Ga., and Crawford High School, Dalton, Ga.; was graduated from the University of Georgia at Athens in 1877; taught school in Dalton, Ga.; studied law; was admitted to the bar in 1878 and commenced practice in Dalton; moved to Texas in 1879 and later, in 1884, settled in Van Zandt County; elected to University of Georgia at Athens in 1877; taught school in Dalton, Ga.; studied law; was admitted to the bar in 1878 and commenced practice in Dalton; moved to Texas in 1879 and later, in 1884, settled in Van Zandt County; elected coucted as a Democrat to the Fifty-seventh Congress to fill the vacancy caused by the death of Reese C. de Graffenreid; reelected to the Fifty-eighth and to the three succeeding Congresses and served from November 4, 1902, to June 14, 1910, when he resigned to become United States district judge of the eastern district of Texas, which office he held until his death in Kerrville, Kerr County, Texas, September 14.

•RUSSELL, SAM MORRIS, (1889-)- U. S. Representative, was born on a farm near Stephenville, Erath County, Texas, August 9; attended the rural schools and the John Tarleton College, Stephenville, Texas; taught school in Erath County, Texas 1913-1918; also engaged in agricultural pursuits; during the First World War served as a private in the Forty-sixth Machine Gun Company, United States Army, in 1918 and 1919; studied law; was admitted to the bar in 1919 and commenced practice in Stephenville, Texas; served as county attorney of Erath County, Texas, 1919-1924; district attorney of the twenty-ninth judicial district 1924-1928; served as judge of the twenty-ninth judicial district 1928-1940; elected as a Democrat to the Seventy-seventh, Seventy-eighth, and Seventy-ninth Congresses (January 3, 1941-January 3, 1947); was not a candidate for renomination in 1946; resumed the practice of law; Democratic county chairman, 1953-1955.

•RUTHERFORD,J.T., (1921-)- U. S. Representative, was born in Hot Springs, Ark., May 30; moved to Odessa, Texas in 1934 and attended the public schools; during World War II served as an enlisted man in the United States Marine Corps 1942-1946 with twenty-eight months overseas; awarded the Purple Heart Medal; captain in the United States Marine Corps Reserve; student at San Angelo (Texas) College in 1946 and 1947 and Sul Ross State College, Alpine, Texas, in 1947 and 1948; attended Baylor University Law School, Waco, Texas, 1948-1950; partner in industrial electrical construction firm; served in the State house of representatives 1948-1952; member of the State senate 1952-1954; elected as a Democrat to the Eighty-fourth, and to the three succeeding Congresses (January 3, 1955-January 3, 1963); unsuccessful candidate for reelection in 1962 to the Eighty-eighth Congress.

S

•SADLER, HOWARD (1924-), lawyer, was born in Port Arthur, Texas on July 19, 1924. A prominent attorney in Port Arthur, Mr. Sadler was educated at the University of Texas, where he received a law degree in 1951. During World War II, he served in the European Theater, and was awarded the Bronze Star and the combat infantry badge. After the war he set up his own practice in Port Arthur, and was a trustee of the local college. He was a director of the Texas Trial Lawyer's Association, and a member of the Amerrican Bar and Texas Bar associations. Mr Sadler is married and has two children.

•SANDERS, MORGAN GURLEY (1878-1956)- U. S. Representative, was born near Ben Wheeler, Van Zandt County, Texas, on July 14; attended the public schools; graduated from Alamo Institute and taught school for three years; owned and published a weekly newspaper; studied law at the University of Texas at Austin; was admitted to the bar in 1901 and commenced practice in Canton, Texas; member of the State house of representatives 1902-1906; prosecuting attorney of Van Zandt County 1910-1914; district attorney of the seventh judicial district of Texas in 1915 and 1916; voluntarily retired and resumed the practice of law in Canton, Van Zandt County, Texas; delegate to many Democratic State conventions; elected as a Democrat to the Sixty-seventh and to the eight succeeding Congresses (March 4, 1921-January 3, 1939); unsuccessful candidate for renomination in 1938; resumed the practice of law in Canton, Texas, until his death; died in Corsicana, Texas, January 7.

161

•**SATANTA** (1820-1878), Indian name *Set-tain-te,* ("White Bear") was a Kiowa chief revered to this day by his people as one of their greatest men. He lived in the High Plains region of Kansas, Texas and Oklahoma. For his eloquence in council he was acclaimed "Orator of the Plains." His ability to combine directness of purpose with grace and wit won the admiration of army officers, even though he was known to be hostile to white laws and white civilization. He was a merciless killer because he knew there was no other way to retain Kiowa lands.

Satanta was one of nine signers of the Medicine Lodge Creek Treaty, Barber County Kansas, October 21, 1867, by which the Kiowas agreed to live on a reservation. In reality, he had no intention of signing away his freedom, but the military might of the United States proved too much for the Indians. Winter was upon them; they were cold and hungry.

Under a white flag of truce, Satanta and *Lone Wolf* came to *General Philip Sheridan's* camp to tell him of their decision to move their people to the Fort Cobb Agency in Oklahoma. *General George A. Custer,* who went out to meet the pair, was so hostile that all the Kiowas hovering in the background ran away. *Custer* took the chiefs as hostages until the runaways returned. They did, but the Kiowas, especially the young braves, found reservation life unbearable. Even Satanta participated in a raid into Texas in May 1871, during which the warriors attacked a wagon train and killed seven teamsters.

Back on the reservation, Satanta and three other chiefs were called before *General William T. Sherman,* who put them under arrest and told them that they would be returned to Texas to stand trial for murder. *Lone Wolf* escaped then; *Setangya* (Sitting Bear) was killed on the way to Texas, so that only Satanta and *Big Tree* were tried and sentenced to death by hanging. Indian agents arranged to have the sentence changed to life imprisonment. Satanta's friends brought about his release, but immediately he participated in new raids. Recaptured, he was sent to prison at Huntsville. Two years later he jumped from a second-floor window to his death.

•**SAYERS, JOSEPH D.** (1841-1929), twenty-first governor of Texas (1899-1903), was born in Grenada, Mississippi, the son of *David and Mary Peete Sayers*. His father, a physician, moved to Texas in 1851 and settled the family in Bastrop County. Joseph studied at the Bastrop Military Institute, but his studies were interrupted when the Civil War broke out and he joined the Confederate Army. He taught school for a while after the defeat, and studied law so that he was admitted to the bar in 1866. In 1873 he was elected to the state senate and in 1875-78 he served as chair of the Democratic state executive committee. In 1879 he was elected lieutenant governor and then was elected to U.S. Congress in 1885. After several terms, Sayers was elected governor of Texas in 1898. He was considered well-versed in Texas history as well as its economy and agriculture, but he was not prepared for the natural disasters that plagued his two terms of office. A state penitentiary was destroyed by fire in 1899, and floods damaged large areas of the state later in the year. Galveston flooded in 1900. However, Sayers was respected for his support of higher education in the state. After his terms as governor, Sayers defended the University of Texas as a regent against *Governor James Ferguson*. Sayers continued to practice law and was chair of the Industrial Accident Board of Texas in 1922-26. He was on the State Board of Legal Examiners at the time of his death at San Antonio.

•**SCHLEICHER, GUSTAVE,** (1823-1879)- U. S. Representative, was born in Darmstadt, Germany, on November 19; attended the University of Giessen; became a civil engineer and was employed in the construction of several European railroads; immigrated to the United States in 1847 and settled in San Antonio, Texas, in 1850; member of the State house of representatives in 1853 and 1854; served in the State senate 1859-1861; elected as a Democrat to the Forty-fourth and Forty-fifth Congresses and served from March 4, 1875, until his death; had been reelected in 1878 to the Forty-sixth Congress; died in Washington, D.C., January 10.

•SHEPPARD, MORRIS, (1875-1941)- (son of John Levi Sheppard), U. S. Representative and U. S. Senator; born in Wheatville, Morris County, Texas, May 28; attended the common schools of Daingerfield, Pittsburg, Cumby, Austin, and Linden; was graduated from the academic department of the University of Texas at Austin in 1895, from the law department of the same university in 1897, and from the law department of Yale University in 1898; sovereign banker, or national treasurer, of the Woodmen of the World for many years; elected first president of the Texas Fraternal Congress in Dallas in 1901; was admitted to the bar and commenced practice in Pittsburg, Camp County, Texas, in 1898; moved to Texarkana in 1899 and continued the practice of his profession; elected as a Democrat to the Fifty-seventh Congress to fill the vacancy caused by the death of his father, John L. Sheppard; reelected to the Fifty-eighth and to the four succeeding Congresses and served from November 15, 1902, to February 3, 1913, when he resigned; elected to the United States Senate on January 29, 1913, to fill the vacancy in the term ending March 3, 1913, caused by the resignation of Joseph W. Bailey, and on the same day was also elected for the term commencing March 4, 1913; reelected in 1918, 1924, 1930, and again in 1936; did not qualify until February 3, 1913, the date of his resignation from the House and served until his death in Washington, D. C., April 9.

•SHIVERS, ALLAN (1907-), thirty-sixth governor of Texas (1949-57), was born in Lufkin, Texas, the son of *Robert Andrew and Easter Creasy Shivers.* He attended public schools in Woodville and Port Arthur, Texas and completed his studies at the University of Texas in 1931 with an A.B. degree, and in 1933 with an L.L.B. He supported his education by working as a shoe salesman. Once admitted to the bar, Shivers joined his father's firm in Port Arthur. He joined other lawyers from 1935 on. In 1934 he was elected to the Texas senate and was reelected twice. In that seat, he supported old age pensions, and wrote the law that extended the Texas boundary for 27 miles into the Gulf of Mexico. He served in the U.S. Army in 1943-45, seeing conflicts in North Africa, Italy, France and Germany before leaving with the rank of major. He was elected lieutenant governor in 1946, and when *Governor Jester* died during his second term, Shivers automatically stepped up to carry his duties. Governor Shivers called for new taxes to pay for the increasing demand for services in the state. For example, facilities for the mentally ill were so inadequate that some patients were housed in jails. More taxes were added in 1951, as the budget grew more complex. The governor also faced declining revenue when the federal government declared the Gulf coast tidelands belonged to the U.S., not Texas. These lands were under lease for oil and gas development, and *President Truman* had vetoed a Congressional bill giving the state the right to lease them in 1946. This issue was one of the most important of Shivers' administration, and it wasn't until 1953 that the lands were restored to Texas. Although many opposed the new taxes on gasoline as well as the governor's program to require safety inspections of cars, Shivers was reelected to serve three full terms. In his last administration, Shivers endorsed a new Commission on Higher Education. He also supported 27 new regulatory laws on the state budget in 1955. He left office in 1957 and continued his alliance with John H. Shary Enterprises in Mission, Texas which is concerned with agriculture, cattle, banking, real estate, and publishing of the *Mission Times.* He continues to reside there with his wife, the former *Marialice Shary.*

•SLAYDEN, JAMES LUTHER, (1853-1924)- (uncle of Maury Maverick), U. S. Representative, was born in Mayfield, Graves County, Ky., June 1; upon the death of his father in 1869 moved with his mother to New Orleans, La.; attended the common schools, and Washington and Lee University, Lexington, Va.; moved to San Antonio, Texas in 1876; became a cotton merchant and ranchman; member of the State house of representatives in 1892; declined to be a candidate for renomination; engaged in agricultural pursuits and mining; appointed as one of the eight envoys to the centennial celebration of the Mexican Republic in September 1910; appointed by Andrew Carnegie as one of the original trustees of the Carnegie Endowment for International Peace in October 1910; president of the American Peace Society for several years; elected as a Democrat to the Fifty-fifty and to

the ten succeeding Congresses (March 4, 1897-March 3 1919);
declined renomination in 1918; managed an orchard in Virginia,
a ranch in Texas, and mines in Mexico; died in San Antonio,
Texas, February 24.

•SMITH, ERASTUS "DEAF" (?-1838), soldier, helped the Texans win the decisive Battle of San Jacinto in 1836. He was born in
New York, but moved with his family while still a boy to
Mississippi. A childhood disease left him deaf, and soon he was
known by that nickname. What he didn't have in one sense he
made up for in the others; his eyesight and sense of smell were
especially keen, and he could often detect an approaching person
or animal before other people. He moved to Texas in 1824 and
joined *Major James Kerr* at Gonzales in 1825. When the Indians
broke up the settlement in 1826, Smith went with *Kerr* to San Antonio, where he lived quietly for several years. He married a
Mexican widow and soon could speak Spanish fluently, which
made him a valuable soldier when the hostilities broke out between the Anglo Texans and the Mexican government. Working
first as a scout, or "spy" as they called it, Smith fought for Texas
independence beginning in 1835. He was soon made a captain. In
1836, he was assigned to *General Houston's* mission at San Jacinto, where the battle was fought that brought down Mexican
General Santa Anna's troops. "Deaf" Smith burned Vince's
Bridge over a bayou so that the Mexican army could not escape
once they entered Texan territory. *Houston* said later that this
action "cut off all means of escape for either army. There was no
alternative but victory or death." After Texas became a
Republic, he led a regiment against the Mexicans at Laredo. A
force of Mexican cavalry met him five miles northeast of town,
and although they withdrew after 45 minutes of fighting, Smith
considered himself too outnumbered to proceed. Smith retired
soon afterwards to the town of Richmond, Texas, on the Brazos
River. He died and was buried there. Deaf Smith County was
named in his honor.

•SMITH, PRESTON (1912-), thirty-ninth governor of Texas (1969-73), was born in Williamson County, Texas, the son of *Charles Kirby and Effie Mae Strickland Smith.* He attended local schools before studying at Texas Technological College (B.S. in 1934). He operated a movie theatre in his hometown. He married *Ima Mae Smith,* and started a family of two children while becoming active in the Democratic Party. He was elected to the Texas legislature in 1944, serving three terms. In 1957, he was elected to the Texas senate. At the side of *John Connally,* Smith was then elected lieutenant governor in 1962, and when the gregarious governor didn't run again in 1968, Smith was able to win by a substantial majority to take his place. He wasn't as colorful or articulate as his predecessor. Although there was a growing Republican movement in the state, and the legislature was sympathetic to business and finance, Governor Smith supported a state minimum wage, and signed appropriations for more vocational training for the poor. Smith won a second term, but soon after he began it, rumors of his involvement in a stock fraud caused a major scandal. The "Sharpstown Affair", named for the town bank that was the location of the dealings, led to the allegation that high-ranking state officials had profited by illegal stock transactions. It was disclosed that among others, Governor Smith and his friend *Gus Mutscher* (speaker of the house). amassed profits totaling more than $300,000. Although he was not impeached or convicted, Smith wasn't reelected for the next term; in fact, most of the incumbents in the 1972 election were not reelected. Smith returned to his home in Lubbock. Since his governorship, he has continued business interests there.

•SMITH, RHOTEN ALEXANDER (1921-) , educator, was born on January 17, 1921 in Dallas, Texas. He was educated at Texas Wesleyan College, University of Texas, University of Kansas, and U.C. Berkeley. Dr. Smith served in the U.S. Army Air Corp. in World War II. After the war he spent a decade as a professor of political science at the University of Kansas. From 1961-67 he was dean of the College of liberal arts at Temple University. Dr.

Smith advised numerous educational and governmental bodies throughout this period. He belongs to the American Academy of Political and Social Science, American Association for the Advancement of Science, American Political Science Association. He has written many books and articles on the subject of government. Dr. Smith is married and has two children.

•SMITH, WILLIAM ROBERT, (1863-1924)- U. S. Representative, was born near Tyler, Smith County, Texas, August 18; attended the country schools, and was graduated from Sam Houston Normal Institute, Huntsville, Texas in 1883; studied law; was admitted to the bar in 1885 and practiced in Tyler until February 1888; moved to Colorado, Mitchell County, Texas, and continued the practice of law; judge of the thirty-second judicial district of Texas 1897-1903; was elected as a Democrat to the Fifty-eighth and to the six succeeding Congresses (March 4, 1903-March 3, 1917); unsuccessful candidate for renomination in 1916; moved to El Paso, Texas, in October 1916 and practiced his profession; appointed United States district judge for the western district of Texas and served from April 12, 1917, until his death in El Paso, Texas, August 16.

•SMYTH, GEORGE WASHINGTON, (1803-1866)- U. S. Representative, was born in North Carolina, May 16; moved with his parents to Alabama, and later to Murfreesboro, Tenn.; attended the common schools and the college at Murfreesboro; moved to Texas, then a part of the Republic of Mexico, in 1828, and settled in the municipality of Bevell, Zavalas Colony (now Jasper County); appointed by the Mexican Government as surveyor, and later made commissioner of titles; delegate to the General Consultation of Texas State convention and a signer of the declaration of independence of Texas in 1836; also a signer of the constitution of the Republic of Texas; appointed by President Lamar, of Texas, commissioner in charge of the boundary line between the Republic of Texas and the United States; engaged in agricultural pursuits; deputy in the Congress of the Republic of

Texas in 1845, and assisted in framing the constitution of the State of Texas in 1845, and assisted in framing the constitution of the State of Texas; elected commissioner of the general land office of the State in 1848; elected as a Democrat to the Thirty-third Congress (March 4, 1853-March 3, 1855); declined a renomination to the Thirty-fourth Congress; served in the Confederate Army during the Civil War; member of the State constitutional convention in 1866; died in Austin, Texas, February 21.

•SOLMS-BRAUNFELS, PRINCE CARL OF (Ca. 1840s), was a German nobleman and early Texas settlement promoter. He was born in the Solms-Braunfels region of Germany, and as a young man became interested in the new Republic of Texas. He and 25 other noblemen formed the Society for the Protection of German Immigrants in 1844 with the purpose of easing the way for settlement in Texas. The group purchased a large tract of land between the Colorado and Llano Rivers, which they thought was near the ocean at Matagorda Bay. They signed up about 440 immigrants who, in return for $240 per family, were to be granted 320 acres of land, a house, tools and food until the first harvest. However, when Prince Carl and the immigrants arrived in 1844, they discovered their land was hundreds of miles away from their landing point at Matagorda Bay. The Prince then set out to find a spot halfway between the coast and the Society's land. He purchased a tract near San Antonio in 1845, but by the time he returned to the colonists, most of the Society's capital had been depleted. Still, about 200 immigrants reached the site of New Braunfels on Good Friday, 1845, and set about building a fort on a hilltop. Although the first winter was particularly difficult since the funds for food had been depleted, Carl continued to try to live in the high style he had been accustomed to in Germany. He received Indian chiefs in his full uniform of the Austrian army. Three months after arriving, however, the prince left the settlement to return to Germany. *John Meusebach* was left to lead the struggling community. (See *New Braunfels*). Prince Carl wrote and published *Texas, a Description of Its Geographical, Social and other Conditions* at Frankfort-am-Main in 1846. The report paints a sorry picture of the Anglo-Americans and Americanized Germans in Texas. Of the latter he wrote, "I admonish my immigrating countrymen to be twice as cautious with them."

•SOUTH, CHARLES LACY, (1892-1965)- U. S. Representative, was born on a farm near Damascus, Washington County, Va., July 22; moved with his parents to Callahan County, Texas, in 1898 and to Coleman County, Texas in 1914; attended the public schools and Simmons University at Abilene, Texas in 1915 and 1916; taught in the Coleman County, Texas, public schools 1914-1920; served as superintendent if schools of Coleman County 1921-1925; studied law and was admitted to the bar in 1925; served as county judge 1925-1931 and as district attorney for the thirty-fifty judicial district 1930-1934; elected as a Democrat to the Seventy-fourth and to the three succeeding Congresses (January 3, 1935-January 3 1943); unsuccessful candidate for renomination in the first primary in 1942 and later withdrew; engaged in the practice of law in Coleman, Texas; member of the State house of representatives in 1947 and 1948; was a resident of Austin, Texas, from 1948 until his death there on December 20.

•STEELMAN, ALAN W., (1942-)- U. S. Representative, Republican, of Dallas, Texas; was born in Little Rock, Ark., March 15; education: Fordyce Grammar School, Fordyce, Ark., 1948-55; Arkadelphia High School, Arkadelphia, Ark., 1955-60; B.A., political science, Baylor University, Waco, Texas, 1964; M.L.A., Southern Methodist University, 1971; fellow, JFK Institute of Politics, Harvard University, 1972; executive director, President's Advisory Council on Minority Business Enterprise, 1969-72; executive director, Sam Wyly Foundation, 1969; executive director, Republican Party of Dallas County, 1966-69; director, L.Q.C. Lamar Society; Pi Sigma Alpha (political science honor society); member of Baptist Church; married Carolyn Findley, 1962, four children: Robin, Kimble, Alan, Jr., and Allison; elected to the 93rd Congress, November 7, 1972.

•STENHOLM, CHARLES W., (1938-)- U. S. Representative, Democrat, of Stamford, Texas; was born in Stamford, October 26; attended Stamford public schools; graduated, Stamford High School, 1957; graduated, Tarleton State Junior College, 1959;

B.S., Texas Tech University, 1961; M.S., Texas Tech University, 1962; farmer; past president, Rolling Plains Cotton Growers and Texas Electric Cooperatives; former member, Texas State ASC Committee; former State Democratic executive committeeman, 30th senatorial district; member, Stamford Exchange Club; past president; Stamford Chamber of Commerce, United Way, and Little League; member, Bethel Lutheran Church; married to the former Cynthia (Cindy) Ann Watson; three children: Chris, Cary, and Courtney Ann; elected to the 96th Congress, November 7, 1978; reelected to the 97th and 98th Congresses.

•STEPHENS, JOHN HALL, (1847-1924)- U. S. Representative, was born in Shelby County, Texas, on November 22; attended the common schools in Mansfield, Tarrant County, Texas; was graduated from Mansfield College, and from the law department of Cumberland University, Lebanon, Tenn. in 1872; was admitted to the bar in 1873 and practiced in Montague, Montague County, and Vernon, Wilbarger County, Texas; member of the State senate 1886-1888; resumed the practice of law in Vernon, Texas; elected as a Democrat to the Fifty-fifth and to the nine succeeding Congresses (March 4, 1897-March 3, 1917); unsuccessful candidate for renomination in 1916; moved to Monrovia, Los Angeles County, Calif., in 1917, and died there November 18.

•STERLING, ROSS S. (1875-1949), thirtieth governor of Texas (1931-33), was born in Anahuac, Texas to *Benjamin Franklin and Mary Jane Bryan Sterling.* He attended public school near his home and worked on the family farm. After 1896, he entered his own business, freighting produce from the farm area to Galveston, Texas. He also owned a general store in Chambers County, and soon had a chain of feed stores in several rural towns. In Batso, he established a bank and soon became interested in the new oil fields. In 1910, he founded Humble Oil and Refining company with two flowing wells. Sterling built the Dayton-Goose Creek Railroad in 1917 and after 1925 he was active in real estate development as well as newspapers in Houston. In

1926 in Houston he built the *Post-Dispatch* building, where he also housed the first radio station there, KPRC. That building became the Shell Building in 1930. In 1927, he was appointed chair of the state highway commission, where he did much to take politics out of the department. Sterling campaigned for good roads in 1930, and was elected governor by a large majority. The Depression had hit, and Sterling provided a relief fund for the unemployed as well as a new child welfare board. In order to control oil production, Sterling invoked martial law in East Texas for six months. He also sought to decrease the amount of cotton grown in order to increase prices. Sterling was not able to be renominated in 1932, and returned to his own oil business, the Sterling Oil and Refining Corporation. He was chairman of the board of that company from 1946 until his death. He was also president of American Maid Flour Mills and an investment company as well as chairman of the board of the Houston National Bank. These last positions were held before his term as governor. Sterling died in Fort Worth, Texas.

•STEVENSON, COKE R. (1888-1975), thirty-fourth governor of Texas (1941-47), was born in Mason County Texas on a farm. His parents were the county surveyor *Robert Milton and Virginia Hurley Stevenson.* He received no formal education but worked on ranches until 1904 and drove a freight team until 1906. Then he moved to Junction, Texas to work as a cashier at the First State Bank. In the meantime, he studied law and was admitted to the Texas bar in 1913. The next year he quit the bank and began work as county attorney of Kimble County. In 1918-21 he was county judge there and gained a reputation for fairness. He returned to Junction and became president of the First National Bank in 1921, serving until his campaign for the state legislature in 1927. He served in 1928-38 representing his district in Austin, and in 1933-37 was speaker of the house. He was elected lieutenant governor under O'Daniel in 1938, and served in that capacity until the governor resigned to take a seat on the U.S. Senate. Stevenson immediately took over his duties, and the next year won the seat in his own right without opposition. Coke was a conservative Democrat who believed in keeping state spending down; this fact, combined with the new abundance after World War II led to a surplus in the state budget. Some of these funds were turned over to the state highway system as well as the state colleges and universities. Stevenson was reelected in 1944, but did not try for another term and left office after serving the longest amount of time of any Texas governor. He managed his ranch near Junction afterwards, and held no other elective office. He did try for U.S. Senator in 1948, but lost by a disputed 80 votes against *Lyndon B. Johnson.* He died in San Angelo and was buried on his ranch.

•**STEWART, CHARLES,** (1836-1895)- U. S. Representative, was born in Memphis, Tenn., May 30; moved to Texas with his parents, who settled in Galveston; attended the common schools; studied law; was admitted to the bar in 1854 and commenced the practice of law in Marlin, Falls County, Texas; prosecuting attorney for the thirteenth judicial district from 1856 to 1860; delegate to the secession convention in 1861; enlisted in the Confederate Army and served throughout the Civil War, first in the Tenth Regiment of Texas Infantry and later in Baylor's Cavalry; moved to Houston in 1866 and resumed the practice of law; was city attorney of Houston 1874-1876; member of the State senate 1878-1882; elected as a Democrat to the Forty-eighth and to the four succeeding Congresses (March 4, 1883-March 3, 1893); was not a candidate for renomination in 1892; resumed the practice of his profession in Houston, Texas; died in the Santa Rosa Hospital, San Antonio, Texas,September 21.

•**STOCKDALE, FLETCHER S.** (1827-1902?), interim governor of Texas (1865), was born in Russellville, Kentucky to unknown parents. He attended common schools and studied law in home state until he was admitted to the bar. Soon afterwards, he moved to Indianola, Texas and opened his own law firm in 1846. He was involved with the opening of new railroads in his areas of the state, and promoted the idea of refrigerated cars for transporting beef. He was elected to the state senate in 1857, and supported secession from the Union in 1861, helping to draft the Ordinance of Secession that year. He was elected along with *Murrah* as Lieutenant Governor in 1863, and supported the Confederate efforts. When *Governor Murrah* fled to Mexico, Stockdale automatically took over his seat for five days, until *President Andrew Johnson* appointed a new officer. After his fleeting term, Stockdale continued his railroad promotion, and was active in the Democratic party. He died in Cuero, Texas, but was buried in Kentucky.

•STRONG, STERLING PRICE, (1862-1936)- U. S. Representative, was born on a farm near Jefferson City, Cole County, Mo., August 17; moved to Texas in 1871 with his parents, who settled in Montague County; attended the rural schools of Montague County, Texas and was graduated from Eastman's National Business College, Poughkeppsie, N. Y., in 1884; county clerk of Montague County 1884-1892; traveling salesman 1892-1898 and 1911-1932; cashier in the National Bank of Bowie, Texas, 1908-1911; member of Texas State Democratic executive committee 1900-1902; unsuccessful candidate for Lieutenant Governor of Texas in 1930; elected as a Democrat to the Seventy-third Congress (March 4, 1933-January 3, 1935); unsuccessful candidate for renomination in 1934; died in Dallas, Texas, March 28.

•SUMNERS, HATTON WILLIAM, (1875-1962)- U. S. Representative, was born near Fayetteville, Lincoln County, Tenn., May 30; moved to Garland, Dallas County, Texas in 1893; studied law; was admitted to the bar in 1897 and commenced practice in Dallas, Texas; elected prosecuting attorney of Dallas County in 1900 and served two terms; president of the district and county attorney's association of Texas in 1906 and 1907; elected as a Democrat to the Sixty-third and to the sixteen succeeding Congresses (March 4, 1913-January 3, 1947); was not a candidate for renomination in 1946; retired from public activities; was a resident of Dallas, Texas, until his death there April 19.

T

•TEAGUE, OLIN E., - U. S. Representative, Democrat, of College Station, Texas; attended Texas Agriculture and Mechanical College, 1928-32; worked way through college while employed with Post Office, Animal Husbandry Department, and the railroad; married former Freddie Dunman of Fort Worth, Texas; three children: James M., John O., and Jill Virginia; volunteered for Army service in 1940; previously served 3 years as enlisted man in National Guard; commissioned second lieutenant in Officers Reserve Corps on finishing Texas A. & M.; commanded First Battalion, 314th Infantry Regiment, 79th Division; was in combat 6 months, wounded a number of times, decorated eleven times; spent 2 years in Army hospital due to combat-incurred wounds; discharged as colonel, infantry, in September 1946 to take seat in Congress; awarded Silver Star with two clusters; Bronze Star with two clusters; Purple Heart with two clusters; Combat Infantryman's Badge, Army Commendation Ribbon, French Croix de Guerre, French Fourragere and Presidential Unit Citation; elected to 79th Congress on August 22, 1946; reelected to succeeding Congresses; chairman of the Veterans' Affairs Committee in the 84th Congress through 92d Congress; member of District of Columbia Committee, 79th Congress through 85th Congress; resigned latter committee to accept seat on Science and Astronautics Committee which was formed in 86th Congress and assumed chairmanship of Science and Astronautics Committee during 93d Congress; chairman of Select Committee which investigated shortcomings of World War II G. I. Bill (it was through these investigations that he was able to author and sponsor the Korean War Veterans Bill Public Law 550); named to Committee on Standards of Official Conduct during 90th Congress; member of Board of Visitors to U.S. Military

Academy, West Point, N.Y., from 1955 through 1971; appointed to Board of Technology Assessment for the Congress in 1972; elected chairman of the Democratic Caucus in January 1971 and reelected unanimously in January 1973; named as Caucus representative to National Democratic Committee in 1972 and reelected unanimously in 1973; named by Democratic Caucus to serve on Committee on Committees for formation of Congress.

•**TERRELL, GEORGE BUTLER,** (1862-1947)- U. S. Representative, born in Alto, Cherokee County, Texas, December 5; attended the public schools, Sam Houston Teachers' College, Huntsville, Texas and Baylor University, Waco, Texas; taught school in Cherokee County, Texas, 1886-1903; member of the State teachers' examining board in 1897 and 1902, and of the State textbook commission in 1903; engaged in agricultural pursuits and in stock raising near Alto, Texas, in 1903; presidential elector on the Democratic ticket of Parker and Davis in 1904; member of the State house of representatives 1898-1902, 1906-1912, 1916-1920, 1930-1932; elected commissioner of agriculture of Texas in 1920, serving by reelection until 1931; elected as a Democrat to the Seventy-third Congress (March 4, 1933-January 3, 1935); was not a candidate for renomination in 1934; resumed agricultural pursuits and resided at Alto, Texas, until his death there on April 18.

•**THOMAS, ALBERT,** (1898-1966)- U. S. Representative, was born in Nacogdoches, Texas, April 12; attended the public schools; during the First World War served as a second lieutenant in the United States Army; was graduated from Rice Institute, Houston, Texas, in 1920 and from the law department of the University of Texas at Austin in 1926; was admitted to the bar in 1927 and began practice in Nacogdoches, Texas; county attorney of Nacogdoches County, Texas, 1927-1930; assistant United States district attorney for the southern district of Texas 1930-1936; elected as a Democrat to the Seventy-fifth and to the fourteen succeeding Congresses, serving from January 3, 1937, until his death in Washington, D.C., on February 15.

•THOMAS, LERA MILLARD, (1900-)- (widow of Albert Thomas), U. S. Representative, was born in Nacogdoches, Texas, August 3; attended Brenau College, Gainesville, Ga., and the University of Alabama; member of the Houston League of Women Voters; first woman elected to Congress from the State of Texas; elected as a Democrat to the Eighty-ninth Congress to fill the vacancy caused by the death of her husband, Albert Thomas, and served from March 26, 1966, until January 3.

•THOMASON, ROBERT EWING, (1879-)- U. S. Representative, was born in Shelbyville, Bedford County, Tenn., May 30; moved to Gainesville, Cooke County, Texas with his parents in 1880; attended the public schools; was graduated from Southwestern University, Georgetown, Texas, in 1898 and from the law department of the University of Texas at Austin, LL. D., 1900; was admitted to the bar in 1901 and commenced practice in Gainesville, Texas; prosecuting attorney of Cooke County, Texas, 1902-1906; moved to El Paso, Texas in 1911 and continued the practice of law; member of the State house of representatives 1917-1921, and served as speaker in 1920 and 1921; mayor of El Paso 1927-1930; elected as a Democrat to the Seventy-second and to the eight succeeding Congresses and served from March 4, 1931, until his resignation on July 31, 1947, having been appointed United States district judge for the western district of Texas; retired as senior judge; is a resident of El Paso, Texas.

•THOMPSON, CLARK WALLACE, (1896-)- U. S. Representative, was born in La Crosse, Wis., August 6; moved to Oregon in 1901 with his parents, who settled in Cascade Locks; attended the common schools and the University of Oregon at Eugene; during the First World War enlisted as a private on May 25, 1917, in the United States Marine Corps; promoted to corporal on December 20, 1917, and served until honorable discharged on December 15, 1918; commissioned a second lieutenant in the Marine Corps Reserve on December 16, 1918; moved to Galveston, Texas, in 1919; engaged in the insurance business until 1920 and the retail dry goods business 1920-1931, when he engaged as a public relations counsel; elected as a Democrat to the Seventy-third Congress to fill the vacancy caused by the death of Clay Stone Briggs, serving from June 24, 1933, to January 3, 1935; was not a candidate for renomination in 1934; resumed activities as a public relations counsel; delegate to the State Democratic convention at Austin in 1936; organized the Fifteenth Battalion, Marine Corps Reserve, in Galveston County, Texas, in 1936 and was called to active duty on November 1, 1940; served as a lieutenant colonel with the Second Marine Division in the Pacific and later returned to Marine Headquarters to head Division of Reserve; promoted to colonel on October 18, 1942, and placed on the retired list on June 1, 1946; resumed his activities as a public relations counsel; elected to the Eightieth Congress to fill the vacancy caused by the death of Joseph J. Mansfield; reelected to the Eighty-first and to the eight succeeding Congresses and served from August 23, 1947, to January 3, 1967; was not a candidate for reelection in 1966 to the Ninetieth Congress; director, Washington, D. C., office, Tenneco, Inc., 1968 to present; is a resident of Galveston, Texas.

•THORNBERRY, WILLIAM HOMER, (1909-)- U. S. Representative, was born in Austin, Travis County, Texas, January 9; attended the public schools; was graduated from the University of Texas in 1932 and from the law school of the same university in 1936; was admitted to the bar in 1936 and commenced the practice of law in Austin, Texas; member of the State house of representatives 1936-1941; district attorney of the Fifty-third judicial district of Texas from 1941 until his resignation in 1942 to serve in the United States Navy; during World War II served in the United States Navy from July 1942 until discharged as a lieutenant commander in February 1946; member of the Austin City Council 1946-1948, serving as mayor pro tempore in 1947 and 1948; delegate at large to the Democratic National Conventions in 1956 and 1960; elected as a Democrat to the Eighty-first and to the seven succeeding Congresses and served from January 3, 1949 until his resignation December 20, 1963; sworn in as United States district judge for the western district of Texas on December 21, 1949 until his resignation December 20, 1963; sworn in as United

States district judge for the western district of Texas on December 21, 1963, serving until he was sworn in as United States circuit judge of the United States Court of Appeals of the Fifth Judicial Circuit on July 3, 1965, in which capacity he is now serving; is a resident of Austin, Texas.

•THORNTON, SUE BONNER (1898-), librarian, was born in Fairfield, Texas. She was educated at the University of Oklahoma and received an MA. from Columbia. She worked in the Oklahoma Public Schools, and as music librarian at Northeastern State College. She is a member of the National Education Association and the Daughters of the American Revolution.

•THROCKMORTON, JAMES W. (1825-1894), eleventh governor of Texas (1866-67), was born in Sparta, Tennessee, the son of *William E. and Elizabeth Webb Throckmorton.* After a public school education, young James followed in his father's footsteps and studied medicine in Princeton, Kentucky. He moved to Collin County, Texas soon afterwards to practice, but the Mexican War led him to the battlefield, where he was a surgeon to *Chevallie's* rangers. He studied law and was admitted to the bar about the same time that he was elected to the state legislature (1851), where he served until 1857. At that time, he was elected to the state senate, and soon became interested in the secessionist movement. He joined the 1861 convention that passed the ordinance of secession, and was one of seven members who opposed the measure to the end. However, he was loyal to Texas and enlisted in the Confederate Army when war broke out. He was brigadier general of Texas's troops at the end of the war. He served on the state senate for four years, but resumed his law practice when the Confederates lost and in 1866 was a member of the Conservative Party and president of the Texas Constitutional convention. Later in the year he was elected governor over the incumbent. Texas was placed under military rule in March 1867 and the governor was obliged to act under several officers who successively held command of his district. The new federal congress did not like the fact that an ex-Confederate held the governorship, and so *General Sheridan* issued an order declaring Throckmorton "an'impediment to reconstruction under the law," appointing ex-governor *Pease* to succeed him. Throckmorton continued his law practice, was elected to represent his district in Congress in 1875-79 and 1883-87, and was successful in his other political attempts. In his later years he was involved in railroading, and carried on this business even while he was on his deathbed at McKinney, Texas.

•TINSLEY, WILLA VAUGHN (1906-), home economist, was born in Garland, Texas on May 28, 1906. She was educated at the Texas Women's University and the University of Minnesota, where she received a doctorate in 1947. Ms. Tinsley taught in the Texas public schools, at the Southwest State Teachers College, and at Texas Tech University. She served as a cirrculum consultant to the Department of the Interior and the U.S. Office of Education.

•TOWER, JOHN GOODWIN (1925-), U.S. Senator, was born in Houston, Texas on September 29, 1925, the son of Joe Z. and Beryl Goodwin Tower. His father was a Methodist minister. John graduated from high school in Beaumont, Texas in 1942, went to college for a year and then enlisted in the U.S. Navy, where he served on an amphibious gunboat in the Pacific. On his return he attended Southwestern University in Georgetown, Texas, and received a B.A. in political science in 1948. In the following years, he worked as a radio announcer in Beaumont and Taylor Texas and later as an assistant professor at Midwestern University in Wichita Falls, Texas. He also returned to school, studying in England and at Southern Methodist University in Dallas where he earned an M.A. in 1953. He resumed teaching at Midwestern University and remained there until 1960.

In 1960 Tower ran against Lyndon B. Johnson in a bid for the U.S. Senate, and although Johnson won, Tower received 41 percent of the vote. Johnson resigned shortly thereafter to take the Vice-Presidency and a new election was called for in April of

1961. Tower ran again on the Republican ticket and won. In the Senate, Tower served on two major committees: Banking and Currency, and Labor and Public Welfare. He was also on the National Republican Senatorial Campaign Committee, and the Civil War Centennial Commission. Tower was reelected to the Senate in 1966, 1972 and 1978. He is chairman of the Republican Policy Committee, chairman of the Armed Services Committee, and a member of the Banking, Housing, and Urban Affairs Committee, and the Budget Committee.

Tower was married to Joza Lou Bullington of Wichita Falls, Texas in 1952. They have three daughters: Penelope, Marian and Jeanne. He later remarried to Lilla Burt Cummings.

•TRAVIS, WILLIAM B. (1809-1836), Texas Revolution soldier, was famous for his last command at the Alamo. He was born to *Mark and Jemima Stallworth Travis* of Red Banks, South Carolina, who moved the family in 1818 to Conecuh County, Alabama. Young Travis attended local schools there, and then began studying law with a judge at Claiborne. Before he was 20, Travis had passed the bar and had set up his own practice. He married one of his former pupils in the school he had taught in, *Rosanna Cato.* The marriage did not work out, however, and in 1831 he left his wife to move to Texas. He settled at Anahuac, a small port at the head of the Trinity River. The following year, the Mexican Revolution began, and Travis was arrested and jailed by the dictatorial commander of Anahuac, *Colonel Bradburn.* When the townspeople forced *Bradburn* to leave town, Travis was released and moved to San Felipe, an important American settlement in Texas. He became active in the growing "war party" that prepared to fight for Americans' rights against the Mexican governors. He also set up a law office in San Felipe and was made secretary of the *ayuntamiento.* As hostilities between Anglo-Americans and Mexicans grew, Travis was at the forefront of a movement to declare Texan independence from the Mexicans. After San Antonio was captured in 1835, Travis and others brought out a scheme to take Matamoras as well, but that proved impossible, and so he served the Texans as a scout. He was eventually promoted to the rank of lieutenant colonel, and since San Antonio was poorly defended, he was sent to the Alamo to assist *Colonel James Bowie* with his small force of men. Many of them fell ill, including *Bowie*, and Travis was left in command of only about 150 men. Declaring "victory or death!" Travis sent messages for aid, but only a few more soldiers came, and they were grossly outnumbered by the Mexicans who encircled the old mission. Still, over 1,000 Mexican soldiers died in the effort to subdue 180 men.

•TURNER, NAOMI COCKE (1903-), biochemist, was born December 19, 1903 in Austin, Texas. She was educated at the University of Texas and Harvard University. She was a member of the American Public Health Association and a specialist in Dental Research. She published over 30 papers in her field of specialty. She was married and had two children,

U

•UPSON, CHRISTOPHER COLUMBUS, (1829-1902)- U. S. Representative, was born near Syracuse, Onondaga County, N. Y., October 17; attended the common schools and Williams College, Williamstown, Mass.; studied law; was admitted to the bar in 1851 and commenced practice in Syracuse, N. Y., in 1851; moved to San Antonio, Texas, in 1854 and engaged in the practice of law; during the Civil War served in the Confederate Army as a volunteer aide, with the rank of colonel, on the staff of Gen. W. H. C. Whiting; appointed by the Confederacy associate justice of Arizona in 1862; presidential elector on the Democratic ticket of Tilden and Hendricks in 1876; elected as a Democrat to the Forty-sixth Congress to fill the vacancy caused by the death of Gustave Schleicher; reelected to the Forty-seventh Congress and served from April 15, 1879, to March 3, 1833; unsuccessful candidate for renomination in 1882; resumed the practice of law in San Antonio, Texas and died there February 8.

V

•**VANDERGRIFF, TOM,** (1926-)- U. S. Representative, Democrat, of Arlington, Texas; was born in Carrollton, January 29; attended public schools in Carrollton and Arlington; graduated, Arlington High School, 1943; graduate of the University of Southern California, Los Angeles, B.A. degree; mayor of Arlington, Texas, 1951-77; past president, Arlington Chamber of Commerce; first president, North Central Texas Council of Governments; first chairman, Tarrant County Convention Center; member, Presidential Commission on Urban Problems, 1967-68; chairman, Texas Urban Development Commission; first chairman, Texas Commission on Intergovernmental Relations; chairman of the board, Arlington Memorial Hospital; past honors include selection as one of Five Outstanding Young Texans by Texas Jaycees and Citizen of the Year in Arlington, Dallas, and Fort Worth; vice president, automobile dealerships; president, insurance agency; married to the former Anna Waynette Smith of Arlington, Texas, 1949; four children: Vanessa (Mrs. Mark Watters), Victor, Valerie, and Viveca; elected to the 98th Congress, November 2, 1982.

•**VAUGHAN, HORACE WORTH,** (1867-1922)- U. S. Representative, was born near Jefferson, Marion County, Texas, December 2; attended the common schools of Linden, Cass County, Texas; studied law; was admitted to the bar in 1885 and commenced practice in Texarkana, Texas, in 1886; city attorney of Texarkana 1890-1898; prosecuting attorney of Bowie County 1898-1906; district attorney for the fifth judicial district of Texas 1906-1910; member of the State senate in 1910; elected as a Democrat to the Sixty-third Congress (March 4, 1913-March 3, 1915); unsuccessful candidate for reelection in 1914 to the Sixty-fourth Congress; appointed by President Woodrow Wilson as United States district attorney at Honolulu, Hawaii, and served from December 22, 1915, to March 22, 1916; United States district judge in Hawaii from May 15, 1916, to April 4, 1922; died in Honolulu, Hawaii, November 10, 1922; interment in Nuuanu Cemetery.

W

•**WARD, MATTHIAS,** (1805-1861)- U. S. Senator, was born in Elbert County, Ga., October 13; was raised in Madison County, Ala.; received a college education in Huntsville, Ala; taught school two years; studied law; moved to the Republic of Texas in 1836 and settled in Bowie, Montague County, and subsequently in Clarksville, Red River County, in 1845; engaged in trading; served a number of years in the Congress of the Republic of Texas; moved to Jefferson, Marion County, Texas; served in the State senate; delegate to the Democratic National Conventions in 1852 and 1856; delegate to the Democratic State convention at Austin in 1856 and served as president; appointed as a Democrat to the United States Senate to fill the vacancy caused by the death of J. Pinckney Henderson and served from September 27, 1858, to December 5, 1859, when a successor was elected; died at Warm Springs, near Raleigh, N. C., October 5.

•**WELLBORN, OLIN,** (1843-1921)- U. S. Representative, was born in Cumming, Forsyth County, Ga., June 18; attended the common schools, Emory College, Oxford, Ga., and the University of North Carolina at Chapel Hill; enlisted in the Confederate Army in 1861 and served throughout the Civil War, attaining the rank of captain in Company B, Fourth Georgia Cavalry; at the close of the war settled in Atlanta, Ga.; studied law; was admitted to the bar in 1866 and commenced the practice of law in Atlanta; moved to Dallas, Texas, in 1871 and continued the practice of his profession; elected as a Democrat to the Forty-sixth and to the three succeeding Congresses (March 4, 1879-March 3, 1887); unsuccessful candidate for renomination in 1886 to the Fiftieth Congress; moved to San Diego, Calif., in 1887 and continued the practice of his profession for six years; moved to Los Angeles, Calif., in 1893; appointed by President Cleveland as United States judge of the southern district of California in 1895, which office he held until January 20, 1915, when he retired; died in Los Angeles, Calif., December 6.

•WEST, MILTON HORACE, (1888-1918)- U. S. Representative, was born on a farm near Gonzales, Gonzales County, Texas, June 30; attended the public schools and the West Texas Military Academy at San Antonio; served with Company C Texas Rangers, in 1911 and 1912; studied law; was admitted to the bar in 1915 and began practice in Floresville, Texas; moved to Brownsville, Texas, in 1917 and continued the practice of law; district attorney for the twenty-eighth judicial district of Texas 1922-1925 and assistant district attorney 1927-01930; member of the State house of representatives 1930-1933; elected as a Democrat to the Seventy-third Congress to fill the vacancy caused by the resignation of John N. Garner; reelected to the Seventy-fourth and to the six succeeding Congresses and served from April 22, 1933, until his death; was not a candidate for renomination in 1948; died in Walter Reed Hospital, Washington, D. C., October 28.

•WHITE, RICHARD CRAWFORD, (1923-)- U. S. Representative, Democrat, of El Paso, Texas; was born in El Paso April 29; educated in Dudley primary school, El Paso High School, University of Texas at El Paso, University of Texas at Austin (B.A. 1946), and University of Texas Law School (LL.B. 1949); member of Phi Alpha Delta and Sigma Alpha Epsilon; during World War II served in the U.S. Marines in the Pacific theater as a Japanese interpreter-rifleman in the campaigns of Bougainville, Guam, and Iwo Jima; awarded the Purple Heart; engaged in the practice of law since 1949; member, Texas house of representatives, 1955-58; El Paso County Democratic chairman, 1962-63; married the former Kathleen Fitzgerald; three sons, Rodrick James, Richard Whitman, and Raymond Edward by Katherine Huffman

White (deceased); member of St. Clements Episcopal Church, El Paso Chamber of Commerce, veterans and civic organizations; member of El Paso County Bar Association, State Bar of Texas; licensed to practice before the United States Supreme Court; trustee and past president, El Paso County Historical Society; elected to the 89th Congress November 3, 1964; reelected to 90th, 91st, 92d, and 93d Congresses.

•WHITMORE, GEORGE WASHINGTON, (1824-1876)- U. S. Representative, was born in McMinn County, Tenn., on August 20; attended the public schools; moved to Texas in 1848; studied law; was admitted to the bar and practiced in Tyler, Smith County, Texas; member of the State house of representatives in 1852, 1853, and 1858; district attorney for the ninth judicial district in 1866; appointed register in bankruptcy in 1867; upon the readmission of Texas to representation was elected as a Republican to the Forty-first Congress and served from March 30, 1870, to March 3, 1871; unsuccessful candidate for reelection in 1870 to the Forty-second Congress; resumed the practice of law; died in Tyler, Texas, October 14.

•WHITMIRE, KATHRYN J. (1946-), mayor of Houston, was born in that city and attended San Jacinto High School, from which she graduated in 1964. Houston during those years had changed from a mid-sized business center of 400,000 people to a metropolis of nearly one-million, and it was growing by the hundreds every day. She began studies at the University of Houston, married James Whitmire in 1966, and graduated with honors in business administration in 1968. Two years later, she earned a master of science degree in accountancy and became a Certified Public Accountant. She and her husband conducted a public accounting practice in the city for a short time; she also was an instructor for the University of Houston Business Department. Afterwards, Whitmire worked with a large CPA firm in downtown Houston, while caring for her ailing husband. Mr. Whitmire died in 1976 after a debilitating struggle with diabetes.

They had no children. In the meantime, Ms. Whitmire became increasingly active in civic organizations and became aware of the growing problems within the city. She ran successfully for City Controller in 1977 and was reelected without opposition for a second term. In a city that had never used the word "planning," Whitmire was urging controls on growth, and a few regulations to put order into the booming metropolis (see *Houston*). She began to consider running for mayor in order to use her business background to solve some of the problems, and decided in 1981 that at the rate the cost of government was going up and the rate at which the bureaucracy was expanding and the quality of services was deteriorating,"it was going to put us in a position in two years that I really wasn't sure I would want to take on the challenge." So she ran in a hotly-contested race against incumbent *Mayor Jim McConn* and others. McConn had become linked to the city's worst problems, and finished third in the election. Whitmire also defeated Harris County *Sheriff Jack Heard* by a margin of 62 percent to 37 percent of the vote. Mayor Whitmire took office in January 1982. She is optimistic about the future, saying that "Houston is a city that offers opportunity."

•WIGFALL, LOUIS TRESVANT, (1816-1874)- U. S. Senator, was born near Edgefield, Edgefield District, S. C., April 21; pursued classical studies; attended South Carolina College (now the University of South Carolina) at Columbia; served as a lieutenant of Volunteers in the Seminole War in Florida in 1835; attended the law department of the University of Virginia at Charlottesville; was admitted to the bar in 1839 and commenced practice in Edgefield, S. C.; moved to Marshall, Texas in 1848; member of the State house of representatives in 1849 and 1850; delegate to the State convention in 1857; served in the State senate 1857-1860; elected as a Democrat to the United States Senate to fill the vacancy caused by the death of J. Pinckkney Henderson and served from December 5, 1859, until March 23, 1861, when he withdrew; served in the Confederate Army during the Civil War; represented the State of Texas in the Confederate Congress; after the war moved to London, England; returned to the United States in 1873 and settled in Baltimore, Md.; died in Galveston, Texas, while on a lecture tour, February 18.

•**WILEY, WILLIAM HENRY** (1913-), educational administrator, was born in Wildhurst, Texas on February 19, 1913. He received his bachelors and Doctorate degrees from Texas A&M University. From 1947 until 1962 he was Dean of Agriculture at the University of Rhode Island. Since 1962 he has been Dean of Agriculture at Clemson University. Dr. Wiley is a member of the American Genetics Association, American Association of University Professors, and other educational organizations. He has written ten scientific papers in his field. Dr. Wiley is married and has one son.

•**WILLIAMS, GUINN,** (1871-1948)- U. S. Representative, was born near Beuela, Calhoun County, Miss., April 22; moved with his parents to Texas and settled in Decatur, Wise County, in 1876; attended the public schools; was graduated from the commercial branch of Transylvania College, Lexington, Ky., in 1890; engaged in the livestock business, agricultural pursuits, and banking; county clerk of Wise County, Texas, 1898-1902; member of the State senate from 1920 to May 1922, when he resigned, having been elected to Congress; elected as a Democrat to the Sixty-seventh Congress to fill the vacancy caused by the death of Lucian W. Parrish; reelected to the Sixty-eighth and to the four succeeding Congresses and served from May 13, 1922, to March 3, 1933; was not a candidate for renomination in 1932 to the Seventy-third Congress; manager of the Regional Agricultural Credit Corporation in San Angelo, Texas in 1933; also engaged in the livestock business and ranching; died in San Angelo, Texas on January 9; interment in Decatur Cemetery, Decatur, Texas.

•**WILLS, JAMES ROBERT "BOB"** (1905-1975), country-western musician and band leader, was best known for his song *San Antonio Rose*. Born in Kosse, Limestone County, Texas, Wills was the oldest of 10 children. His father was an accomplished fiddle player and taught his son to play the mandolin and fiddle at an early age. In 1913, the family moved to Memphis, where Wills remained until 1929. He resettled in Fort Worth and began to play the fiddle for a living. He joined guitarist *Herman Arnspiger* to form the Wills Fiddle Band, and then in 1930 took on vocalist *Milton Brown* to perform at local dances and shows. A flour company hired the group along with others to form the Light Crust Doughboys, which performed on radio shows under the direction of *Wilber Lee "Pappy" O'Daniel* (O'Daniel later became governor of Texas). *Tommy Duncan* replaced *Brown* and in 1932, Victor Records recorded the Doughboys. However, Wills and *O'Daniel* didn't get along, and Wills was fired in 1933 for arguing and ecsessive drinking. Taking Duncan and his brother *Johnnie Lee Wills* with him, he formed the Bob Wills and His Texas Playboys band and began touring Texas and Oklahoma. The band became a regular feature on the Tulsa, Oklahoma radio station, KVOO. They became so popular that in 1935 Brunswick Records in Dallas signed them up for a session. In the next few years, the band grew from 13 members to 18, so that it rivalled the "Big Bands" of *Benny Goodman* and others of the early 1940s. Wills wrote the song *San Antonio Rose* within 30 minutes before a show in 1940 and performed it before a receptive audience. Many other people liked the tribute to the Lone Star State, and when it was first recorded it sold a million copies. Wills put his career on hold for a few months in 1942-43 when he joined the army. When he was discharged for health reasons, Wills moved to California, and upon discovering that the Big Bands era was fading, formed a smaller version of the "Texas Playboys'." He toured the nation with general success until 1962, when he suffered his first heart attack. Another attack came in 1964, but he was able to resume performing by the next year. In 1968, Wills was elected to the prestigious Country Music Hall of Fame in Nashville. "The King of Western Swing" was honored by the state of Texas in 1969 for his contribution to the state's music. One day after the ceremonies, Wills suffered a paralyzing stroke that left him an invalid for many months. By 1972, he was partially recovered and was able to perform again from his wheelchair. He joined several other country-western musicians in 1973 to make an album for United Artists. However, Wills suffered a stroke after the first day. He remained in a coma for 17 months until his death. Wills' music has been revived by several musicians in recent years. In 1976, a "Greatest Hits" album of his band's music was released, and his song "San Antonio Rose" has been sung by many prominent artists and celebrities, including *Bing Crosby*.

•WILSON, CHARLES, (1933-)- U. S. Representative, Democrat, of Lufkin, Texas; was born in Trinity, June 1; attended public schools of Trinity, Texas, graduating from Trinity High School, 1951; while a student at Sam Houston State University at Huntsville, Texas, was appointed to the U.S. Naval Academy; graduated from the Academy, 1956, with B.S. degree; served in the U.S. Navy, 1956-60, with rank of lieutenant; elected to the Texas House of Representatives, 1960-66; elected to the Texas Senate, 1966-72; lumber yard manager; married Jerry Carter, 1963; elected to the 93d Congress, November 7, 1972.

•WILSON, JAMES CLIFTON, (1874-1951)- U. S. Representative, was born in Palo Pinto, Palo Pinto County, Texas, June 21; attended the public schools and Weatherford (Texas) College; was graduated from the law department of the University of Texas at Austin in 1896; was admitted to the bar the same year and commenced practice in Weatherford, Texas; assistant prosecuting attorney of Parker County 1898-1900 and prosecuting attorney 1902-1908; chairman of the Democratic county executive committee 1908-1912; moved to Fort Worth in November 1912 and served as assistant district attorney of Tarrant County until July 1913; United States attorney for the northern district of Texas from July 1913 to March 1917; elected as a Democrat to the Sixty-fifth and Sixty-sixth Congresses and served from March 4, 1917, to March 3, 1919, when he resigned; appointed by President Woodrow Wilson as United States district judge for the northern district of Texas, serving from March 13, 1919, until his retirement in 1947; died in Fort Worth, Texas, August 3.

•WILSON, JOSEPH FRANKLIN, (1901-1968)- U. S. Representative, was born in Corsicana, Navarro County, Texas, March 18; attended the elementary school at Corsicana; at the age of twelve moved to Memphis, Texas (in the Panhandle), and attended the public schools until 1916; during the First World War enrolled at Peacock Military College, San Antonio, Texas, from September 1917 to June 1918 and at Tennessee Military Institute at Sweetwater from September 1918 to June 1919, advancing through the grades to first sergeant; graduated from Baylor University Law School, Waco, Texas, in 1923; was admitted to the bar the same year and commenced practice in Dallas, Texas; delegate to the Democratic National Convention in 1936; chairman of the Dallas County Democratic Executive Committee 1942-1945; district judge of the criminal district court of Texas in 1943 and 1944; elected as a Democrat to the Eightieth and to the three succeeding Congresses (January 3, 1947-January 3, 1955); was not a candidate for renomination in 1954; appointed judge of Criminal District Court No. 1, Dallas, Texas, in 1955, in which capacity he served until September 1968, when he retired due to illness; died in Dallas, Texas, October 13.

•WOOD, GEORGE T. (1795-1858), second governor of Texas (1847-49), was born in Georgia to unknown farmers. He attended public schools in his native Randolph County, and as a young man fought Indians at the Battle of Horseshoe Bend. He was a merchant for a time, and then was a member of the Georgia state legislature. He moved to Texas in 1839 and soon became prominent in public affairs, serving for several years in the Texas Congress and Senate while it was independent. He also operated a cotton farm in present San Jacinto County. He was a member of the state constitutional convention, and in 1846 he raised a regiment for the Mexican War, gaining considerable distinction as a soldier. He was a member of the state senate before his election to the governorship. His administration was concerned with building up the new state which had been preoccupied with war for so long. He authorized construction of public buildings, organized counties and townships, and presented reforms as well as rang up a state debt of over $5 million by the end of his term. At the close of the Mexican War, the federal government had wanted to establish authority over the Sante Fe country in Texas. This region was reorganized into the territory of New Mexico, much to the displeasure of many Texans. Wood was indecisive over what to do about this territory, while many of his fellow statesmen called for secession from the U.S. if the Santa Fe were not returned to Texas. He was not reelected governor, but returned to his plantation. He was buried near Pointblank, Texas.

•WOOTEN, DUDLEY GOODALL, (1860-1929)- U. S. Representative, was born near Springfield, Greene County, Mo., June 19; moved in infancy with his parents to Texas during the Civil War; attended private schools in Paris, Texas, and was graduated from Princeton College in 1875; attended Johns Hopkins University, Baltimore, Md., and was graduated from the law department of the University of Virginia at Charlottesville; was admitted to the bar in 1880 and practiced in Austin, Texas; prosecuting attorney of Austin 1884-1886; moved to Dallas, Texas, in 1888; judge of the Dallas County district court 1890-1892; presidential elector on the Democratic ticket of Cleveland and Stevenson in 1892; member of the State house of representatives in 1898 and 1899; delegate to the National Antitrust Conference at Chicago in 1899; member of the executive council of the National Civic Federation in 1900; delegate to the National Tax Conference at Buffalo in 1901; elected as a Democrat to the Fifty-seventh Congress to fill the vacancy caused by the death of Robert E. Burke and served from July 13, 1901, to March 3, 1903; unsuccessful candidate for renomination in 1902; continued the practice of law in Seattle, Wash.; served as special judge of the superior court at various times; delegate to the National Rivers and Harbors Congress in 1912; delegate to the National Conservation Congress in 1913; appointed a member of the State board of higher curricula by the Governor in 1919; author of several historical works and numerous articles in literary and law periodicals; tendered the position of professor of law at the University of Notre Dame, Notre Dame, Ind., in 1924, and served until his health forced him to take leave of absence in November 1928; died, while on a visit, in Austin, Texas, on February 7.

•WORLEY, FRANCIS EUGENE, (1908-1959)- U. S. Representative, was born in Lone Wolf, Kiowa County, Okla., October 10; moved to Shamrock, Texas, in 1922; attended the public schools, the Texas Agricultural and Mechanical College at College Station in 1927 and 1928, and the law school of the University of Texas at Austin 1930-1935; was admitted to the bar in 1935 and commenced practice in Shamrock, Texas; member of the state house of representatives from 1935 to 1940, when he resigned, having been elected to Congress; served as a lieutenant commander in the United States Navy from December 1941 to August 1942, while a Member of Congress; elected as a Democrat to the Seventy-seventh and to the four succeeding Congresses and served from January 3, 1941, until his resignation, effective April 3, 1950; appointed an associate judge of the United States Court of Customs and Patent Appeals, Washington, D. C., and served from April 4, 1950, to May 4, 1959; appointed chief judge May 4.

•WRIGHT, JAMES C. JR., (1922-)- U. S. Representative, Democrat, of Fort Worth, Texas; was born December 22 in Fort Worth; son of James C. and Marie Lyster Wright; educated in public schools of Fort Worth and Dallas, Weatherford College, and University of Texas; enlisted as a private in the United States Army in December 1941, flew combat missions in B-24s in South Pacific, awarded D.F.C. and Legion of Merit; four children - Jimmy, Virginia Sue, Patricia Kay, and Alicia Marie; partner in trade extension and advertising firm; served in Texas Legislature and two terms as mayor of Weatherford; served during 1953 as president of League of Texas Municipalities; lay worker in Presbyterian Church; elected to the 84th Congress, November 2, 1954; reelected to each succeeding Congress; married to former Betty Hay of Fort Worth; active in sponsorship of legislation for water pollution abatement, interstate highways, economic development, and Latin American relations; named most respected member of House in survey conducted among colleagues by U.S. News & World Report in 1980; elected majority leader, 95th, 96th, 97th, and 98th Congresses.

•WRIGHT, JAMES C. JR., (1922-)- U. S. Representative, Democrat, of Fort Worth, Texas; was born December 22, in Fort Worth; son of James C. and Marie Lyster Wright; educated in public schools of Fort Worth and Dallas, Weatherford College, and University of Texas; enlisted as a private in the United States Army in December 1941, flew combat missions in B-24s in South Pacific, awarded D.F.C. and Legion of Merit; four children - Jimmy, Virginia Sue, Patricia Kay, and Alicia Marie; partner in trade extension and advertising firm; served in Texas Legislature and two terms as mayor of Weatherford; served during 1953 as president of League of Texas Municipalities; lay worker in Presbyterian Church; elected to the 84th Congress November 2, 1954; reelected to the 85th, 86th, 87th, 88th, 89th, 90th, 91st, 92d, and 93d Congresses; married to former Betty Hay of Fort Worth; active in sponsorship of legislation for water pollution abatement, interstate highways, economic development and Latin American relations.

•WURZBACH, HARRY MCLEARY, (1874-1931) (uncle of Robert Christian Eckhardt)- U. S. Representative, was born in San Antonio, Texas, May 19; attended the public schools, and was graduated from the law department of Washington and Lee University, Lexington, Va., in 1896; was admitted to the bar the same year and commenced practice in San Antonio, Texas; during the Spanish-American War volunteered as a private in Company F, First Regiment, Texas Volunteer Infantry; after the war moved to Sequin, Texas, in 1900 and continued the practice of law; prosecuting attorney of Guadalupe County 1900-1902; judge of Guadalupe County 1904-1910; elected as a Republican to the Sixty-seventh and to the three succeeding Congresses (March 4, 1921-March 3, 1929); successfully contested the election of Augustus McCloskey to the Seventy-first Congress; reelected to the Seventy-second Congress and served from February 10, 1930, until his death; delegate at large from Texas to the Republican National Convention at Cleveland in 1924; died in San Antonio, Texas, November 6.

•WYATT, JOSEPH P. JR., (1941-)- U. S. Representative, Democrat, of Bloomington, Texas; was born in Victoria, October 12; attended the public schools; graduated from Bloomington High School, 1960; attended Victoria College; B.A., University of Texas, 1968; graduate work, University of Houston Law School; served in the U.S. Marine Corps Reserve, 1966-70; served on the staffs of: Texas State senator William N. Patman, U.S. Congressman Clark W. Thompson, and Vice President Lyndon B. Johnson; auditor, Texas Alcoholic Beverage Commission, Austin, Texas; director of community affairs, Safety Steel, Inc., Victoria, Texas; member, Texas House of Representatives, 1971-79; chairman, Texas House Ways and Means Committee, 1974-78; served on: Southern Legislative Conference and National Conference of State Legislatures; Outstanding Young Man of the Year, Victoria Jaycees, 1976; member: St. Patrick's Catholic Church, Victoria Chamber of Commerce, Port Lavaca Chamber of Commerce, Mid-Coastal Sportsmens Club, Victoria Jaycees, Texas Farm Bureau, McNamara-O'Conner Historical and Fine Arts Museum, Ducks Unlimited, and Pi Kappa Alpha Fraternity; elected to the 96th Congress, November 7, 1978.

Y

•YARBOROUGH, RALPH WEBSTER, (1903-)- U. S. Senator, was born in Chandler, Henderson County, Texas, June 8; attended the public schools of Chandler and graduated from Tyler (Texas) High School; attended the United States Military Academy, West Point, N. Y., in 1919 and 1920 and the Sam Houston State Teachers College, Huntsville, Texas, in 1921; taught school for three years in Delta and Martin Springs, Henderson County, Texas; spent one year working and studying foreign trade and international relations in Europe, mostly in Germany as assistant secretary for the American Chamber of Commerce in Berlin; served in the Thirty-sixth Division, Texas National Guard, from private to staff sergeant, 1923-1926; worked as a harvest hand in the wheat fields of Oklahoma and as a tank builder in the boom oil town of Borger, Texas, in 1926; graduated from the University of Texas Law School in 1927; was admitted to the bar and commenced the practice of law in El Paso, Texas; served as assistant attorney general of Texas 1931-1934; wrote Texas' first underground water conservation law in 1931; member of the original board of directors of the Lower Colorado River Authority in 1935; unsuccessful candidate for State attorney general in 1938; lectured on land law at University of Texas Law School in 1935; served as district judge of the Fifty-third Judicial district, Austin, Texas, 1936-1941, and for three years was presiding judge for the third administrative judicial district; during World War II served in Army ground forces with the Ninety-seventh Infantry Division with combat duty in Europe and with occupation forces in Japan from February 1, 1943, until discharged as a lieutenant colonel in June 1946; author; member of Texas Board of Law Examiners 1947-1951; unsuccessful for the gubernatorial nomination in 1952, 1954, and 1956; elected as a Democrat to the United States Senate in a special election April 2,

199

1957, to fill the vacancy caused by the resignation of Price Daniel and served from April 29, 1957, to January 3, 1959; reelected in 1958, and again in 1964 for the term ending January 3, 1971; unsuccessful candidate for renomination in 1970; is a resident of Austin, Texas.

•YOAKUM, CHARLES HENDERSON, (1849-1909)- U. S. Representative, was born near Tehuacan, Lincoln (now Limestone) County, Texas, July 10; attended Larissa College in Cherokee County and Cumberland College; studied law; was admitted to the bar in 1874 and commenced practice in Emory, Rains County, Texas; served as prosecuting attorney for Rains County in 1876; moved to Hunt County in 1883 and continued the practice of law in Greenville; district attorney for the eighth judicial district 1886-1890; member of the State senate 1892-1896; elected as a Democrat to the Fifty-fourth Congress (March 4, 1895-March 3, 1897); continued the practice of law in Greenville, Texas, until 1900, when he moved to Los Angeles, Calif.; returned to Texas in 1904; died in Fort Worth, Texas, January 1.

•YOUNG, JOHN ANDREW, (1916-)- U. S. Representative, was born in Corpus Christi, Nueces County, Texas, November 10; attended the Incarnate Word Academy and Corpus Christi College-Academy; St. Edwards University, Austin, Texas, B.A., 1937 and from the University of Texas School of Law, LL. B., 1940; was admitted to the bar in 1940 and commenced the practice of law; volunteered for service in the United States Navy in 1941, before Pearl Harbor, served in all theaters of war, and was separated from the service in 1945 as a lieutenant commander for physical disability incurred in line of duty; awarded the Presidential Unit Citation for service beyond the call of duty; assisted county attorney of Nueces County in 1946; assistant district attorney of Nueces County 1947-1950; county attorney in 1951 and 1952; county judge of Nueces County 1953-1956; elected as a Democrat to the Eighty-fifth and to the six succeeding Congresses (January 3, 1957-January 3, 1971).

Z

•**ZAHARIAS, MILDRED "BABE" DIDRICKSON** (1914-56), athlete, was born in Port Arthur, Texas and became active in sports at an early age. She was an All-American basketball player while in high school in 1930, and in 1932 won 5 of 10 events at the American Athletic Union (AAU) Women's Track and Field Tournament. Her skill in track and field games enabled her to participate in the 1932 Olympics in Los Angeles, California in 1932, where she set a new record in the javelin throw (143 feet), and a U.S. record in outdoor 80-meter hurdles. "Babe" Didrickson left the track after high school to take up golf. She regained amateur status and by 1935 was competing for titles. Twelve years later she was considered the leading women golfer in the nation, having won 17 titles. When she won the British Women's Amateur Golfing Tournament, she was the first American to do so. In the meantime, Didrickson had married *George Zaharias*, a wrestler. Mrs. Zaharias gained professional status as a golfer in 1948 and the next year was named the Outstanding Woman Athlete of the Century by the Associated Press, which was made even more outstanding by the fact that the century wasn't half over yet. It was during another winning season in 1952 that the golfer began to feel ill. Her illness was diagnosed as cancer, and she underwent surgery that gave her a remission for several years. She was able to win the U.S. and All-American Opens in 1954, and to write her autobiography, *The Life I've Led*, in 1955. The next year, however, she underwent surgery again, and grew increasingly ill until her death at Galveston, Texas.

•ZARAFONETIS, CHRIS JOHN DIMITER (1914-), physician and educator, was born in Hillsboro, Texas on January 6, 1914. He was educated at the University of Michigan and received his M.D. in 1941. Dr. Zarafonetis was professor of medicine at both the Univesity of Michigan and Temple University. He served as advisor to the Department of Defense on a variety of medical questions. The doctor is a member of many professional societies and the author of over 140 articles on medical subjects. He is married and has one child.